T0381122

Awakening: Finding the Light

LAURA LYNN

BALBOA.PRESS
A DIVISION OF HAY HOUSE

Balboa Press books may be ordered through booksellers or by contacting:

Balboa Press
A Division of Hay House
1663 Liberty Drive
Bloomington, IN 47403
www.balboapress.com
844-682-1282

Bible Scripture is taken from King James version of the Bible, public domain.

Author Photo Credit: Lindsey Ramdin

Print information available on the last page.

ISBN: 979-8-7652-5359-5 (sc)
ISBN: 979-8-7652-5360-1 (e)

Balboa Press rev. date: 07/17/2024

Contents

Contents

Dedication

This story of awakening is dedicated to all who supported my journey of enlightenment.

To my parents, Tom and Lynn, for their unconditional love and support of every dream I have ever had in my life. I am so grateful to call you mine.

To my children, Annabelle and Dustin, for their patience, excitement and encouragement while mom was working on her book. You both are truly the 'light' of my life, I love you so much.

To my cousin, Dr. Rev. Mary Linn Clarke, for her immense and selfless contribution to my education and love of mediumship, meditation and metaphysics. I will always strive to make you proud.

Finally, to Dr. Rev. Karen Brooks and the College of Inner Awareness, Metaphysical and Spiritual Studies. Thank you for blessing me with the knowledge I needed to be grounded and successful, for without you, this book wouldn't have been possible.

Introduction

*"The meaning of life is to find your gift. The
purpose of life is to give it away."*

– Pablo Picasso

Since I was young, I have always had an emotionally sensitive soul. Literally, just *feeling* things so deeply can get quite intense for individuals like me. I often would take things to heart and allow my energy to be drawn into negative people or situations. It wasn't until later in my life that I would learn how I (and many, many others) can quite literally absorb the energy of people, places and animals around us. I had heard of this thing called the "aura" but had not truly understood what it was. As I approached my thirties, I was already sick and tired – of *being* sick and tired! Chronic illnesses, depression, high anxiety and exhaustion all plagued me in my late teens and throughout my twenties. The medications just weren't doing it for me – they helped at times, but I felt like a zombie. I needed something else, something... *more.* Something or someone that would show me the light and bring back my smile. I wanted that peace in my mind, body and soul. Then, just like that, they were brought into my life to help me begin the journey of my awakening.

I know I have many purposes during this lifetime, and one of those was to write this book. My enlightenment has been one of the hardest and most fulfilling journeys in my life up to this point. After falling far from grace, and God, I finally found out that all the answers I was seeking, were already within me. I just had to stop, turn off the noise of life and listen. It was in that quiet place between all the chaos that I found what I was looking for and I began to wake up from the darkness and find my light again.

Now my life's purpose is being fulfilled one day, one moment and one breath at a time. I figured out - that I did not have to figure it all out! I was free and in control of whatever I wanted my next step in life to be. The feeling was liberating and terrifying all at once... now that I have all this time left to *live*, what do I do next? Whatever. My. Soul. Wanted. And I did just that. You can too – just join me in my journey and I promise somewhere in these lines you will find your truth. Your purpose. Your way.

The time has come for you to awaken.

Chapter 1

Depression, Doctors and Drugs, Oh My!

> "Depressed means you need deep rest from the
> character you've been playing in the world."
>
> – Jim Carrey

I cannot help but believe that every single human being has coped with depression or anxiety at some point in their life. Whether we want to admit this, is a whole other story and I am about to tell you mine.

My stressed and negative mental health battle kicked into full gear around seventh grade when my hormones started to peek, and life began to feel a lot more serious. This was the point where what others thought of me really mattered to my heart and soul. Or at least it felt that way in the moment. What I realized now looking back on it, I was so deep into my own ego and mind, I couldn't see anything other than what I wanted to see. Which makes sense for a thirteen-year-old, but I was not the average teen and I knew that. I recognize now that my sensitivity was extraordinary compared to most. I felt like I was constantly being judged and had to watch my every move. Kids have a way of doing that to one another, especially as we go into our middle and high school years.

At the time it seemed detrimental and consuming, wondering what other people were saying behind my back. Like their opinion was going to rock my entire world when I showed up for school the next day. Most days I didn't want to go to school, and I wouldn't because usually what I was feeling would come true. I would think or focus on something negative for so long, it consumed me and became a reality. So, as I continued into my later teens and early 20s, this trend of being concerned with what other people thought of me would almost devour me. Not only that, but dealing with very loving and supportive, yet stressed parents and having family issues at home – life felt like it was spinning out of control.

I even tried counseling at a very young age beginning after my Papa passed away, I felt like I had a lot of sadness with nowhere to go. So, when I was around ten years old, the school counselor came to our class letting us know that if we were every feeling 'big feelings' and needed to talk, she was always there to help us through it. We began meeting weekly and she was an angel to me that made me feel better every time I spoke with her. She brought a sense of softness, understanding and peace to my life that no one else could at the time. After I moved out of elementary school, we couldn't keep our meetings so once again I felt lost and lonely. I began going to a psychologist later at the age of sixteen to help me cope with all the craziness still occurring in my life. She was a great soul too and seemed to help at first, but at this point the answer to all my sensitivity issues was to be medicated.

I guess it made sense though, especially to all the doctors that I have seen in life between psychologists and psychiatrists. I cried constantly describing my life to them, and I was in this deep, dark place that I couldn't seem to find my way out of. My feelings were legitimate with the environment I was experiencing, but my reactions to all of it were too much. My emotions were so overwhelming it was as though I couldn't even keep control over how I was feeling. Of course, things are different for me now that I have enlightened and matured, but looking back on it, it was almost debilitating how tremendous my sensitivity was to the people and events going on around me in my life. My mind was making things to be way worse than what they truly were. I kept focusing on what was going wrong in my life instead of what was happening that was *good*.

Even though counseling did have its benefits, there was so much more to what I was feeling than what their education or experience could provide to help me. I needed something more to help me navigate my way through life and allow me to feel 'normal' again. It's so disappointing how easy it is for doctors in these modern times to hand out anti-depressants and anti-anxiety medications. I do believe that the universe sends us doctors and scientists who have the purpose to develop these types of drugs that do help many people. But at the same time, I think they are overly prescribed to the empaths and sensitive souls of the world. It seems like they are an easy answer, now I have learned that holistic treatment such as meditation, yoga and reiki are such healthier options for souls like mine.

At first, the anti-anxiety medication I was being prescribed at sixteen years old seemed like it was helping. I didn't feel so edgy or anxious all the time. No more crying endlessly for hours over a break-up or fight with someone I cared about. No more anger over being mistreated by others or what they were saying about me. Nothing. Literally. I felt nothing. Yet was that really the answer to all my issues? To put a mask over all my emotions with this zombie type feeling of numbness to everything around me. I was not me anymore, I was just functioning. I was simply existing in this cloudy fog I called my life. The doctor's orders needed to be followed as I trusted them, and so I kept taking what was prescribed.

When I decided in my senior year to stop taking the pills, old Laura seemed to resurface. The good, the bad and the extremely anxious. Feeling much better and actually happy that I could physically cry again; it was like I was human once more. Yet the thoughts and emotions were back to being so overwhelming they overpowered me again. This time it was worse than ever, situations seemed to be drowning me and I just wanted out. No more thoughts, no more pain, no medications and no more doctors. If you could get inside of my head, it probably would have looked like I was running 100mph on a hamster wheel!

Self-harm came along with these feelings of helplessness. I would cut my arms just to feel real pain instead of the emotional pain that was holding me hostage. It was focusing the hurt on something else so I could *stop thinking and feeling so much.* I know everything happens for a reason, and it was a blessing I stopped taking those meds when I did and threw them out. This is because not long after stopping them, I would attempt to take my own life by suicide. (By the way, on a healthy medical note, I weaned off the meds safely as instructed by my physician. Sudden withdrawal or stopping these types of medications quickly is very dangerous, so please be aware and talk to your doctor first.)

I'll never forget that morning before school when I began taking random pills and waiting to see what would happen. This is why I said it was a blessing to get off them when I did, overdosing on that type of medication is highly lethal. I got to school and just started ingesting them every 15 to 20 minutes waiting to pass out and get the attention I was desperately seeking. Before that moment could take place, the guidance counselor called me down to her office to meet with my best friend at the time. She brought us in because my friend had reported me to the office due to my emotional outburst at her in front of many other people the day before. I was hurt in such a way that no friend should ever feel hurt, and I was beyond angry with her treatment of me and disrespect. I had found out my boyfriend was cheating on me with her, and I just lost it. It was like my entire world was caving in, how could they do this to me? It felt like the worst moment ever in my life and I wasn't going to get over it. So, I just wanted to end it all.

As we sat in her office discussing the situation I continued to keep my head down and quietly cry while we were trying to talk it through. I remember the counselor looking at me with a lot of concern, able to tell I was extremely depressed and not my normal self. It was when my words began to slur, and my head started to bob that she finally asked if I was alright. I told her I wasn't and that I had been taking pills all morning and I just wanted to die. You can imagine the energy of the room shifted dramatically as she frantically called my parents to come pick me up. I refused the ambulance because I didn't want everyone in the whole school to know about what happened. It was a blessing when we were called down to her office, otherwise I could have overdosed in class, and everyone would have found out. Plus, if I hadn't said anything and let those meds sink into my system longer, I wouldn't be writing this book.

After I got to the ER with my father, I immediately had to have my stomach pumped with charcoal by having a tube inserted (without numbing) down my throat. They tried to make me drink it before using the tube method, but it was too hard for me to ingest orally. Everybody was scrabbling around me in such a hurry trying to help my body stop the medications from taking my life. The doctors and nurses did their jobs well, but I read it in their faces that I was being a nuisance or irritating to them. In that moment, I felt like a gigantic failure and even more lost as

I left the emergency room with my dad. "Why would you DO that??" he kept asking me. I knew the main reason was because my boyfriend and friend betrayed me. I was completely devastated and heartbroken. But I couldn't tell my dad that and all the other reasons I hated my life at that moment. So much pressure at eighteen, finishing high school and figuring out what to do when you are done. Love and relationships with friends feel like the biggest deal in the world, it was everything to me at that age.

I needed someone to talk level with me, but no one did. After the incident, I honestly do not believe my father or mother even knew *how* to talk to me, because mental health was not something considered or discussed growing up in the 1950's and 60's. My parents are amazing parents, but they had their own moments of feeling emotionally overwhelmed. How can you help or even begin to understand a suicidal child, when you have never discussed or learned about the importance of positive mental health in your lifetime? This type of situation is usually kept secret by families, not wanting to 'look bad' to others or people in the community.

Many times, when a family member commits suicide, they will not mention the manner of death. To them this protects that loved one's image and they are trying not to cloud their good name. Over my years I have found that some of the most wonderful, happy souls choose their own departure. The ego of poor self-image is toxic, and part of the reason suicidal people feel so worthless and frowned upon. When what we really need more than ever is love and lots of it. So, we keep up the smile, to avoid the shame or look of worry coming from family and friends. Now we are in 2024 and it genuinely is time to start talking about suicide openly and honestly. We do not need to hide it anymore; we need to make every soul feel heard with love and support. Not feel any sort of shame or awkwardness by sharing their deepest thoughts or feelings. Let's confront it and start beating it before it even begins. I am certain that many people who have known me most of my life may read this book and never knew this part of my story. The old me would have been way too consumed in what they thought of my suicidal attempts. The new me says, "other people's opinions of me are none of my business!" If anything, I pray that discussing these attempts I made in my life will support others to get the help they need. Or maybe assist a person to better understand how to help their child, sibling, parent, friend, coworker or partner who feels the same way I did.

Realistically, I attempted taking my life just to get someone to notice me – not to die necessarily. Although it felt like either way would have made me feel much better at the time. The initial we love you and support came from the closest around me that knew what happened. But after a few days went past, the topic went away and life continued. Nobody attempted to speak to me more deeply about what happened. To me, I did not try to talk about it either because it felt as though more feelings of shame and embarrassment would just come up with the discussion. So of course, I went on feeling alone, humiliated and ashamed of myself. It is important to mention here that I in no way blame my parents for their shortcomings in handling this situation with me, they were always so good to me. I had a wonderful and loving childhood, but unfortunately, they were clueless as to how to help me fight this battle in my mind. They tried and wanted to, but I was good at hiding the pain behind my goofy personality and big smile. As I mentioned before, this is the face of suicidal people. We seem so happy, funny and outgoing, while suffering silently inside. So, I put on my best face and moved forward, only for the plague of suicidal thoughts to return a year later.

My second attempt was during my first year in college and trying to take the world on solo for the first time in my life. I had found out that same boyfriend at the time (ugh, yes... my codependent, sensitive and naïve soul returned to him) was back home cheating on me, AGAIN. At this point the anger, rage, fear, sadness and heartbreak were too much for me to bear. I was living with a roommate who was away for the weekend, so without anyone watching I took any pills I could find in my apartment – vitamins, ibuprofen, etc. and just laid on the floor, waiting to pass out. Would I die, would I live? I didn't care, just wanted to make life go away. Hoping my roommate would miraculously come back for something she forgot and find me to come to my rescue. Then she would see how desperate I was for attention... but this did not happen. No one came and no one knew what I had done or what was happening.

As a laid on the floor crying for what seemed like an eternity waiting for anything to happen, a close friend from home happened to call and she could tell I was completely incoherent. I told her what happened and that I was so incredibly sad. Being the caring friend she was (now a nurse), she immediately drove for an hour to get me and take me back home to my parents. By then, most of the meds had processed and I was stable enough to walk and talk as normally as I could. There was no way I could tell them why I came home, I just said that I was alone that weekend and wanted to come hang out with friends. The next day, I checked into the ER secretly to make sure I was not poisoned and would recover okay from all the things I took. The last thing I wanted or needed was for my parents to find out and I would just feel like a complete failure all over again.

After being checked in and stating the reason I was there was attempted suicide, they took me back into an isolated room that had nothing but a bed in it. The walls were dirty and scratched, there wasn't even a TV for me to watch while I waited. No extra chairs in the room, no special medical tools on the wall, not even a rubber glove box. I then realized I was in what I assumed was "the crazy person room". They did not want me to try and hurt myself again. I sat there all alone and waited for multiple doctors and counselors to come in and ask me the same rhetorical questions everyone else had asked me for the last three years. Why do you want to hurt yourself? Do you do any drugs? Is there any abuse in your family?

Everybody was making me feel like a medical science project, instead of treating me like a nineteen-year-old girl who was just completely lost and trying to call out for help. They saw I had a little cocaine in my system from the previous weekend of bad decisions, and immediately wrote me off. I was far from being an addict or having a drug problem. It was more like a trial-and-error stage I was in while between the ages of 18 and 20 years old. I experimented with a lot of things to get 'high' and feel better, but none stuck because I did not want to become an addict and the relief was always temporary. So, for them to judge me because of that, was just wrong. I can honestly say that in both attempts, the treatment at either medical facility made me feel as though I was irrational and just another immature teenager who was hormonal and/or on drugs.

Next, they called my parents because even though I was legally an adult, they needed to contact a family member for support and make them aware of what happened. So, my dad showed up not long after I arrived, and the feeling of shame came back to me seeing him in this position once again. My poor loving father, so concerned for me yet so embarrassed wondering the same thing everyone else did. WHY LAURA? I could tell he was slightly annoyed but tried to hide it and show he still loved me. He didn't know how to help me, and I see that now looking back on it. No matter his efforts, once again, I left the hospital feeling even more alone, stupid and out of place than ever. What was wrong with me? Why couldn't I just make better choices and be normal mentally?

It was shortly after I made my second suicide attempt, that my close friend's brother followed through with his overwhelming thoughts and decided to leave this earthly experience we call life. I loved him like my own brother as she was like a sister to me, so the loss hit extremely hard. He was so animated, comical and full of life whenever I saw him. I knew he was so loved, but I also knew *exactly* how he felt when I heard the devastating news of his departure. It was the reaction of the family and seeing them in pain that I began to realize I *had* to get better. I would never want my loved ones to be in so much sorrow and feeling like they should of, could of or would have done something else to help.

The one true and bittersweet blessing at the time was a nurse who was dating my best friend's dad at the time – the same best friend that had just lost her big brother. She was also working as the nurse in the ER after my second attempt and was the one who checked me in and admitted me. I remember her being completely shocked when I appeared at the registration counter and told her why I was there. Laura the bubbly, happy go lucky girl I know – wants to KILL herself? But WHY? Because… even the happiest people in the world can be the most deeply affected by emotions because of how hard we feel. Empathy can be beautiful and extremely draining if you do not know how to manage it.

I had not seen her since my attempt and as I stood at the casket of this young man with so much light and love in his life – she came up next to me, put her arm around me and held me. As the two of us stared down upon him, her next words hit me in a way that I needed to hear years ago to wake up. "He was so loved Laura. Do you see how his actions hurt so many people that truly loved him? He felt so lost, but we did not know he felt that way and he would not reach out to us. Make a list Laura, make a list of *everyone* you know that loves you. Then the next time you want to take your life, imagine their reaction to hearing that you have died – the incredible pain that it causes. You make that list and call every name on it until you are okay and truly know how loved you are. Please don't leave yet, you have so much to do." Looking down upon my friend's brother while she softly and firmly gave me the guidance I so desperately needed to hear, was life changing. From that day forward, I would never attempt to take my precious life again. I had too much to do – and here I am, doing it.

For it was in that moment, that I began to awaken…

Chapter 2

Energy and the Amazing Aura

"The ego doesn't know that the source of all energy is within you, so it seeks it outside.

– Eckhart Tolle

Energy as defined by Merriam-Webster has multiple meanings: 'the capacity of acting or being active', 'a usually positive spiritual force', 'vigorous exertion of power', 'usable power such as heat or electricity' and finally – 'a fundamental entity of nature that is transferred between parts of a system in the production of physical change within the system and usually regarded as the capacity for doing work'. So many different meanings in the dictionary, but to me energy is *much* more complex compared to those and has a larger impact on our daily lives. We use it, give it or always receive it, and it has much more significance than we tend to recognize or understand.

Many of you reading this may relate to how I feel energy, for instance when I meet a new person for the first time, I will almost immediately know if I like them or not. Why? How? Quite simply, you're reading their vibrations. Every single one of us has intuition and psychic abilities, but most do not even realize when they are using them. I truly believe the saying is true that "your vibe attracts your tribe." Who you share your energy with regularly will have a massive influence on you mentally, spiritually and physically. You may even relate to this intuitive feeling when walking into an event or environment and getting a feeling of positive and uplifting vibes making you feel good. Or it may be the opposite, you may become uneasy and feel like the energy is totally off.

Or have you experienced what felt like the greatest day ever and then come home to share it with someone, only they have had the exact opposite type of day? They are feeling angry, hurt or sad and suddenly – you do too and now your awesome day has disappeared. You are totally sucked into that person's vibes and starting to feel their misery. That is a direct example of how our energy is distributed and shared by those around us. It could also happen the other way around and you could be having a terrible day, then that one positive person with great energy turns your frown upside down! Either way understanding energy, how it's transmitted and how to keep it or block it was vital in my awakening and enlightenment process. It would also become extremely helpful to me as I began my development as a psychic medium.

In metaphysical and spiritual terminology, the energy we carry around us is called the 'aura'. It isn't just a spiritual term either, the aura has been proven to exist scientifically in the realm of quantum physics. So, when you share a close physical distance with someone, you are in each other's energy, or aura. Think about it... can you recall a time where you were in another person's presence (or animal's) and you could actually *feel* their emotion? Their laughter made you smile, their anger made you uncomfortable or their crying made you sad too? These are all examples of empathy and sharing energy.

A personal experience I had before fully comprehending how energy travels from one person to another, happened when I lived in Florida and started studying how to do hands-on-healing using therapeutic touch. It was a part of my development, and I was just starting to learn the basics of healing, energy and the aura. Well, my close friend at the time was in a moment of deep despair because of an alcoholic she was dating that was causing her much grief. I loved my friend dearly and my empathy for her was overwhelming as I did not want to see her so sad and upset. I offered to give her a healing to try and lift some of the heaviness of her emotions. After we finished, I could tell she felt better, so that made me feel better too in the moment. When I got home, something minor that happened suddenly triggered me out of nowhere and I began to cry feeling overwhelmed with the situation. My husband at the time asked what was wrong with me and he said to me, "Ever since you've come back from your friend's house, you have been super emotional and edgy. Why?" After a moment of thinking about it, he was right! I didn't even put the two together until he said that to me. Suddenly, I came to the realization that not only had I forgotten to protect myself with light before I began the healing, but one vital step when you're finished healing someone is to wash your hands. Energy is magnetic and it literally sticks to you. So, when you are a spiritual healer or Reiki practitioner, it's an important part of the process to wash your hands and rid yourself of that person's energy. I quite literally absorbed, held and carried her energy home with me and took it from her. As soon as I realized this, I took a long shower and asked for the energy to be released from mine and I started feeling better almost right away! It was an important lesson to learn in my development as a healer, but also just as a sensitive person in general. We need to learn how to differentiate our energy from somebody else's in order to elevate feeling what they are feeling.

Being a sensitive and anxious person most of my life, I tend to put a lot of emotion and stress behind my never-ending thoughts. Doctors would diagnose me as having high anxiety or ADHD. I honestly didn't even consider what anxiety really meant or where it came from back in my teens and twenties. I just knew that it defined me, because I always was in that constant state of worry which drained me mentally and physically. This resulted in me then having anxiety's counterpart – depression. I am quite certain that everybody has had anxiety or depression at some point in their life or has experienced it with somebody they love. Understanding energy and how it works can make such a dramatic impact on your mental health when dealing with these types of diagnosed illnesses.

As discussed in chapter one, this type of intense, anxious behavior reached its peak with me between the ages of 16 and 19 years old. It would get to a point where my brain would be racing with vivid thoughts of situations and scenarios that hadn't even happened yet. After keeping myself up all night, my brain and body decided to crash because they were completely exhausted. The depression that set in would just make me want to sleep all day. Now I look at "lazy and moody" teenagers in a whole different way, because looking back at myself, I get it. Most put so much energy into their feelings and need for approval combined with hormonal changes and social pressures, it drains them. Mentally and physically, anxiety and depression will take their toll - especially with teens. Schoolwork, love life, friends, sports, and to top it off in most recent years - social media. I can see how quickly it consumes young people and their energy gets wasted by putting it towards unimportant people or events. Even adults are getting sucked into this modern phenomenon by allowing videos and stories online to influence their energy daily lives. Without even knowing if a post or article has any truth to it, we respond in frustration, anger and irritation at what is being said. Starting online battles with keyboard warriors just to defend something or someone is needlessly taking away our precious energy. Once again, identifying there's issues with what, where or who we are spending our time on is the first step towards completely changing your life.

Regarding feeling energies around us, some of the most sensitive souls are children and animals. Both know when they feel fear or happiness coming from those around them. Younger children are especially gullible and empathetic to the thoughts or actions of others; it is out of their control when they react to the energy around them. If they are acting out or misbehaving, stop for a moment and reflect on the vibes happening around them. Is it a calm environment with positive vibes or could they be reacting to chaos and discord? We cannot always believe that the child needs to be disciplined, changed or made to feel guilty of their reactions when they are simply responding to the environment and aura of others around them. It is *us* (the adults or parents) that usually need to change *our* energy. The divorcing parents whose emotions are so intense they can't see how their words or actions are directly affecting their kids. The teacher whose stressful life at home gets carried into the classroom. Children are unable to monitor and manage how to react to these energies, they just do so naturally and intuitively.

This is the same with animals. They get an instinctive feeling using their senses, and they react. Some flee trying to find peace and solitude, while others bite or fight back in defense of themselves or their babies. Truly, I believe that they are ones who can read our energy better than any other living being on earth. Since they can't strike up a friendly conversation with people, they

16

are always using their intuition to feel the energies around them. Have you ever looked in an animal's eyes and just *knew* what they were trying to tell you? I have seen many videos to demonstrate that telepathy and energy reading is how they communicate with humans and with other animals around them as well. This is why dogs tend to growl if they sense a threat around them. Some people give off a better "vibe" or energy and animals feel more secure around them. Or you may be that person that freaks out at any type of animal or insect around you, so in turn, they may feel that fear in your energy and try to flee or attack. Either way, if you're not sure about an animal's intentions or reactions towards you, keep that in mind and try to remember to calm yourself down. They can feel what you are feeling, so the more relaxed the aura is the better the connection will be felt for both of you.

So, now you may be asking yourself the question – "How do I control the energy coming off of my aura?" The answer is: manage your thoughts and reactions consistently. It's really that easy, well maybe not at first, but it will become that way the more often you do it! Like learning anything else in life, some things take time and others come along more quickly. Starting by just acknowledging the energy coming off your own aura is the first step. When you realize that you are having a moment of irritation and your communication is starting to get more fierce or loud, change it. Leave the room or environment and take a moment for yourself to breathe. Notice your thoughts, ego and mind are getting the best of you – and in that moment of realization – you are awakening.

By taking responsibility, and changing your own thoughts or actions, you are making progress toward a much more peaceful existence. We all make mistakes and owning up to them can prove to be quite difficult for many of us. Yet, once this can be accomplished, it makes the future brighter and easier to manage energetically. Stop yourself in that moment of anger or frustration and ask yourself, what energy am I putting off and how is it affecting myself and those around me? It can also be a good time to understand and figure out where the emotions in your reaction came from. Healing the root of the issue will change how you react to it happening again in the future. That acknowledgment is a huge step in your enlightenment process.

Now, look ... I get it. Some days you cannot help it and you just want to be angry and mad! Not caring one bit of who feels it around you and releasing that energy to anyone in your path. Family, coworkers or even the checkout person at the grocery store. True growth is when you do notice, start to care and take responsibility for your actions - your awakening has begun. When at our most irritable and anxious, separate your aura from all those souls nearby you. Take a few moments to reflect upon what has occurred to you to feel this way and how you can change your thoughts and energy towards the issue or person that was aggravating you.

The most important part to remember is a phrase that took me a long time to accept, but once I did, it clicked and stuck. This is that nobody *makes* us feel anything - we *choose* to react to it. This is a hard truth to accept, but it is a reality regardless of anyone's acceptance. Our brains have been conditioned this way our whole lives. Does this phrase sound familiar? "Well, this person said/did this to me and it made me so angry. It hurt me deeply and now because of what they did I'm going to be in a bad mood. They ruined my day." It could be true that they hurt you, but it was *you* who chose to react to their words or actions with anger, sadness, stress or worry. We have total control over how we respond or react to others in our environment. It's time to stop blaming everyone else for our reactions and take control of them ourselves. They may have a strong influence to encourage the reaction out of us, but we are the ones who will ultimately decide if we will spend our energy by responding or not. I do love the phrase "it's not worth my energy" because I find it to be so healthy and mindful of the situation.

The next question I get asked often is "how can I protect or rid myself from the energy of others?" Well, this can be accomplished in a few different ways. One of the most efficient ways I have found to rid yourself of stress or anxious energy around you is to exercise. Certain people prefer vigorous forms of exercise to expel any negative or unwanted energy within their mind, body and soul. Others may want to try slower exercises like yoga, tai chi or long walks. Anything you can do to redirect your heavy mental energy into something more physically positive or worthwhile is a great approach to take when managing stressful moments. Clean out a closet, play with a pet or child, make a to do list or write in a journal. No matter what it is, shift your energy and you will begin to feel lighter, then you have more clarity and focus to handle the situation.

The other method I use daily and most often to protect my energy, is to mentally and spiritually surround myself in a white light. (Ha. I know this method may sound a little unconventional and out there for some of you, but I promise it works. Give it a try and see how your day changes!) As a medium, you learn this during your development to protect yourself from negative entities or energies around you. The amazing part is that it works in the daily physical world too! There are various ways to surround yourself with white light, and all of them are done using visual imagery. One way is to imagine yourself inside an egg made of a beautiful, warm healing white light. See yourself surrounded and protected in your shell. Another way is to keep a hula hoop under/near your side of the bed or wherever you sleep. Then when you awaken each day, step into the hoop and imagine it is a ring of white light. Bend down and lift it up over your head while you imagine it surrounding you and shielding you. Flip the hoop over your head to complete your circle of light and place it back down at your feet. Once again visualize yourself surrounded and protected. No matter which method you choose, physical or mental, the result will remain the same. You see and feel a beautiful illumination of peace and protection all around you. The main purpose of the light is to create an invisible barrier to protect your aura from any outside energies. I like to think of it as a boomerang, and that whatever energy is cast towards it just reflects it right back off to its source. Acting like a shield of safety mentally, physically and spiritually.

Here are a few situations when putting white light around yourself, or others, can really help you out in certain circumstances.

Situation 1

Have you ever been in line at the grocery store, shopping mall etc. and found yourself next to the most irritable and nasty person ever?! Doesn't matter who it is, they are ready to unleash fury on all who cross their path that day? This type of scenario is when I remember to turn on my white light ASAP. My soul goes into high alert because I don't want that energy anywhere near my aura. As you surround yourself for protection, you may also focus on sending out love and light to that troubled soul as well. We don't know what someone else is going through at home or what types of personal challenges they are dealing with. Always choose kindness and positivity when sending energy to someone, regardless of if we feel they are good or bad people. Just wish them well and go back into your little personal bubble of white light, so all will be right!

Situation 2

You must go visit an ill family member or friend in a hospital or hospice. This type of scenario is where it can be vital to protect yourself with white light. Being completely open in this type of environment with no protection can drain your energy quickly and take days to recover. It is also important, and possible, to visualize the light around others with you as well. Now they will also be protected in their the mind, body and soul from absorbing the lower energy of sickness or departure. Again, send out your beautiful vibes to uplift and heal others while keeping the entrance gate to your aura closed with your white light. As I stated earlier, it is always encouraged to wash your hands or shower after encountering anyone physically or mentally ill as it cleanses the energy off your aura.

Situation 3

When you are attending a large, crowded event with lots of people, it can get overwhelming having so many individual auras around you. Especially depending on the mood of the event! It's fun to go to a concert and share in that happy, excited energy of those around you. Other times you may be on that crowded bus in the city, at a work convention, amusement park or other busy atmosphere where many energies get mixed up into one space. At times, the energy of these bigger events or being around lots of other people is too much for those who are very sensitive. You may want to exit the environment and be by yourself for a moment, that's because you're feeling the overpowering energy of the crowd. If that is the case, take a deep breath and surround yourself in that light for protection and to ease the anxiousness. Remember you are in control!

Now that we understand the energy and aura, and how powerful it is, you may begin to think about what you are attracting in your life. One thing that we must let go of completely in our life is fear. The next chapter will discuss releasing fear from your energy and replacing it with confidence, power and strength.

For it was when I found my true inner strength, and
let go of my fears, that I continued to awaken ...

Chapter 3

Fear: Let. It. Go.

"There is no illusion greater than fear."

– Lao Tzu

One thing that surprised me as I was studying the topic of 'fear', is that from it stems all the negative emotions or energy we experience. Rage, sadness, anxiety, depression, irritability, anger ... all of it comes from fear. It has been taught that this is also coming from the ego, which puzzled me even more. In simple terms, the ego is defined as "the opinion that you have of yourself." (Merriam-Webster) In spiritual terms, the ego is a misperception of who you really are. A false sense of identity. Something that many may not realize is that our fears are completely conditioned by our past. So, to recognize why we are afraid, we need to understand their origins and where they come from. Which is either stored in our subconscious mind (such as phobias) and/or influences made during our childhood.

Can you think back to when you were younger, and a situation occurred that created a great fear inside of you? Are you still scared of these things to this day? For example, if somebody has a traumatic experience with an animal such as being bitten by a dog, then as they grow into an adult, they will most likely have a fear of dogs. Or someone who may have been hurt or injured in a house fire may become extremely afraid of being around a flame. On a more emotional level, impressions during our childhood or relationships could lead us into a fear of abandonment. I cannot tell you how many times I've heard people say, "I always find the same type of person to date that is toxic and a narcissist. So, I'm done looking for a relationship because they're all the same and all I ever do is get hurt so I'd rather be by myself." Or many times I hear that "I was terribly abused growing up and I have a hard time trusting anyone now because of it."

Projecting that type of fear into your future is only going to create sadness and depression, leaving you physically drained and unmotivated. You do not have to fear that situation happening again just because it happened in your past. Using it as a guide or tool will help you create healthy boundaries in your life from the difficult lessons that were learned. Accepting a traumatic or tough past can create a warrior of strength within you and humble you. For others, the fear of 'what if it happens again' can drain and defeat you, the choice is yours. Most of the people I have met that have been through the hardest or most damaging experiences in their life either come out with a powerful, kind and enlightened soul or others may succumb to it and lead a life of repeated negative patterns or behaviors.

Phobias tend to show themselves from a deeper subconscious level of fear. I recall taking a course and reading in it that our fear of the dark most likely stems from the days of cavemen. As we sought shelter in the dark for many long years, before we discovered the creation of light. This could also explain having distress in certain situations like claustrophobia in small spaces or being frightened of heights. All of this fear is most likely stored from past lives into your subconscious mind and carried with you throughout your journeys here on Earth, until you face them.

Most of what I have learned about fear and understanding it came from the College of Inner Awareness, Metaphysical and Spiritual Studies (CIAMSS). They state that there are two types of fear: irrational and rational. Irrational fear is what's most common among people and it will mess with your mental state. It's a destructive fear and an unnatural response to threats. This type of fear takes away your peace of mind causing anxiety, depression and worry. All of these are classified as irrational fears.

Rational fear is a natural response to a genuinely difficult situation or threat. Your senses and intuition become heightened. For example, someone breaking into your home, getting into a car accident, having a very ill loved one in the hospital, etc. would naturally create a natural reaction of fear. Now doing something like checking your locks thirty-two times before bed as a ritual, in fear of something bad happening, is irrational. Do you recognize the difference?

Fear can be so destructive to the human mind, body, and soul - this is why it is so imperative to identify and overcome it. It kills people's dreams, their hope and faith, it can make you physically/mentally sick, and can even age you. You may not be living your life to its full potential, because you want to stay safe even if it means you will be miserable. Keeping everything "normal" allows people to feel protected and secure, even if they are unhappy. Fear can hold you back and even hinder you from doing things that you very well know you can do. You can have all the potential and all the talent in the world, and still be held back from abundance and greatest, because you are afraid.

So, if this is you, I want you to ask yourself: how is this being supportive of my dreams and goals in life? How is this beneficial to not do what you truly want to do? Sometimes we just need to take life on and not let our worries hold us back. One definition of fear that's been shared throughout the ages is that it is "False

Evidence Appearing Real". It is a state of mind or consciousness, and it truly can be changed. When you think about your life are you very content and happy with your situation? Or would you like things to be improved, like there's a bigger purpose for your life than what you're currently doing?

It's very important that we pay attention to our inner conversation and how we are talking to ourselves daily. Some of my favorite lyrics come from a song called "The Search" by an artist named NF. He raps:

"The point I'm makin' is the mind is a powerful place.
And what you feed it can affect you in a powerful way.
It's pretty cool, right? Yeah, but it's not always safe.
Just hang with me, this will only take a moment, okay?
Just think about it for a second if you look at your face
Every day when you get up and think you'll never be great
You'll never be great.
Not because you're not but the hate
Will always find a way to cut you up and murder your faith."

A lack of confidence and debilitating anxiety keeps people from doing things that they truly want to do in life. They just cannot see themselves beyond the situation that they are currently in. I have come to realize that every successful person worked through their fears by making sure their inner dialogue was positive and uplifting. Nobody graduates college by thinking, I do not think I will finish or I'm not sure that I am good enough. The ones who do succeed are the ones who say, "I'm going to do this, I am going to graduate and become everything I can see myself being with my full potential. The sky is the limit, fear will not hold me back!"

Could you imagine if Muhammad Ali said, "I am the worst"

instead of "I am the greatest"? Would he have been so successful in his career if he did? Or when Bill Clinton was just a child and went into the White House, he said "One day I'm going to become president of the United States." I fully believe if he would have felt being President was something impossible to accomplish, he would of never made it to that position. People with ambition, motivation and drive get themselves to where they want to be faster, because they believe they can do it. How they do this by letting go of their fears, finding their inner strength and pushing through. Whatever energy you are putting out, the universe will respond with the same.

I can recall some of the most important times of my life when I had to overcome my fears. One of them being when I finally left my marriage and recognized that my children's happiness was dependent on my own. It was time for me to be independent and free, I was done being afraid, I could do it. I had been with my then husband since we were very young, we practically grew up together and grew apart together as well. It was so hard for me to see myself outside of that relationship and moving on in life without him.

My mom always told me, "Laura, it's better to have one happy parent, than two miserable ones." When she said that to me, it really made so much sense and reaffirmed that it was time to let go. At that point I had gained a lot of weight, I was so depressed and finding my irritability coming out towards my children, family and friends. It was like the negative environment had taken over me and I was just spreading it out everywhere. Remember the previous chapter on energy? Yes, everybody was feeling mine and I was feeling anything but happy. It was like a nonstop game of volleyball with my husband, playing with a ball that was always filled with frustration between the two of us.

It's extremely difficult to push down and ignore how you're

feeling when you have been hurt, especially when you already are an emotionally sensitive and empathetic soul. What was making it worse (without us or them knowing it at the time) was those around us constantly being 'worried' about our marriage and sending us that vibration of fear energy in their thoughts, words or actions. This is understandable, as it comes from a place of love and just wanting the best for both of us, but what is in their mind is it is sad and disappointing, which comes from – fear. Divorce and separations from loved ones whose energy is no longer loving, kind and respectful – is *necessary*. Each time I hear about this type of situation with someone, I tell them "Congratulations!". This is because it takes a lot of courage to face your fears, cut someone off and make the big changes needed for your personal happiness.

At the same time I was going through this epiphany and ready for big changes in my life, my cousin Mary Linn (the family medium and spiritualist minister), moved just a few miles down the road from me in Florida. Shortly after her arrival, she came to me asking if I was ready to develop as a psychic medium. At first, I laughed at this idea and said "I don't know Mary Linn, how will I ever make a living out of that? She said, "I have and that's not for you to figure out right now, right now it's time for you to learn and your studies with me will take about two in a half years until you're ready. You need to learn meditation and one day you will be ordained a minister like me. This is the right way to do it, from the bottom up."

At first when I heard her say all of that, I was thinking to myself, she must be crazy! I know she's a very talented medium in my family, but there's no way I could leave behind being an elementary school teacher. My mind immediately began recalling all the years of college education, supplies I bought, multiple hours of working and training I had accomplished, to just to completely start over … and as a psychic medium?! How would people look at me? Would I even be able to do this?

Excitement, anxiety and all the different types of emotions you could possibly feel were going through me in that moment. I've always known I had a higher purpose, and a strong attachment to spirit and angels, but I was just in *fear* of the change, how would it even be possible? How could it work? The answer was with me the entire time. I didn't have to figure out *how* to get there, I just knew that's where I wanted to be. It wasn't going to happen overnight, but allowing myself to dream of this new reality was the first step in conquering my fear and creating the career and life that I was destined for.

Once I began developing with Mary Linn, I became more and more comfortable with my intuitive and mediumship development. I recognized I was able to do things far beyond anything I could ever see myself doing. The more I continued to release my fears, visualize and see success happening for myself, the universe just kept paving the way for me. The time had come for me to leave behind my current career, my marriage, my FEARS - and completely start over. Anyone can understand how scared I was, but if I didn't push through being afraid, I wouldn't be sitting here writing this today. Ending my marriage and completely changing my occupation was the scariest time I've ever faced in my entire life. Now that I look back, I am so incredibly grateful that I took the leap of faith, got over my fears and found my true purpose.

If you are somebody who struggles with fear and has a hard time finding the strength to get you there, you most likely suffer from its most common form which we discussed earlier, called anxiety. It can be crippling and overwhelming if not addressed and recognized. Anxiety is created from feeling or thinking of unwanted future outcomes and trying to control something that hasn't even happened yet. Our minds like to generate imaginary scenarios of things going wrong. This can be especially true for parents or caregivers, not wanting harm to come to their loved ones. I can feel a few of you chuckling while you're reading this, recognizing it's describing yourself on most days. Yeah, no worries my friends! I am absolutely, positively, undoubtably certain we have all experienced anxiety in one way or another at some point in our lives.

It can be felt in a few different ways for most people, depending on how they express or feel it. The first type of anxiety is repression, when people bury the anxiety deep into their mind, body and soul and hold it there. Allowing all the thoughts to race through their minds while they chew on their nails or bob their leg up and down incessantly. I've been able to physically see the repressed anxiety sitting inside of people without them saying a word. Without releasing this hectic energy, it has nowhere to go which leads to illness physically and mentally.

Another way people experience anxiety is through worry or guilt. Always being concerned about the well-being of others, or if you said or did something wrong. This is something I've been working on as a mom, and with my own mom, for many years. We have a tendency to *worry* about our children or family/friends and their safety and life choices. This is the exact opposite of what we want to do for ourselves and our loved ones. Whenever my mom tells me that she is worried about me, I immediately respond to her and say "Don't say that mom! Send me your love not your fear." Remember from the last chapter, energy is transferable and contagious. If someone is sick or in a hard spot in life, and you're constantly sending worried energy their way, you're just adding more of that fear to their aura, rather than helping them heal. I love the term 'no worries', it a great way to accept what is and release any fears of the situation.

Guilt can be another fear that we carry with us for a lifetime if we don't learn to let it go and forgive ourselves. We all make mistakes, but holding on to the guilt of something you said or did, will only eat away at you from the inside out. Again, this too may cause you to have physical illness, as fear increases adrenaline and cortisol production in our bodies. If you have found yourself carrying heavy guilt lately or even for many years, please remind yourself that you are a spirit energy having a human experience. Making mistakes and learning lessons is what we are here to do. It doesn't have to be a life sentence, and taking accountability by owning up to your words or decisions is the most healing thing you can do for yourself or others.

The last way people express anxiety is through hysteria. Again, I am sure we all have been there or know someone who reacts this way in our lives. Where even the thought of something going wrong sends them into a complete downward spiral mentally, imagining all the ways it will unfold. Panic or anxiety attacks are symptoms of hysteria. The mind starts racing with so many different scenarios and the "what if" thoughts, that the body can't keep up with it. The heart races, we may begin to sweat or pace all due to letting our thoughts make us hysterical. Many have found that taking a few large, deep, relaxing breaths multiple times is a great way to calm down this type of reaction.

Now that we understand a little bit more about our fears and where they come from, let's discuss some support things we can do to overcome these fears and find your peace. Here are six important steps to start with:

1. <u>Face your fear.</u>

One of the most valuable and powerful ways to overcome your fear is to face it. When I say this, instantly my mind is taken to a story of a young girl who was a surfer in California named Bethany Hamilton. She had her arm bitten off by a shark one day while surfing, which

31

was one of her biggest passions in life. I was so shocked to read in the article that she immediately went back out into the ocean and got on her board as soon as she got the OK from the doctors that she was well enough to surf again. She didn't want to live in fear of something that she loved to do so much just because a once in a lifetime tragedy occurred. Shark bites are not a regular occurrence, so for her to have a fear of always getting bitten by a shark would have been 'irrational'. My advice to you is if you're scared of something, do it. If you're scared of being in a relationship because you've been hurt before, go ask someone on a date. The musician Travis Barker was in a plane crash years ago that took the lives of all the passengers except for him. For years, he has had a great fear of flying, but just recently with his wife by his side, he overcame his fear and got on an airplane again. Remember that fear is only in your mind, and that your true strength comes when you decide to take it head on and face it.

2. Accept that fear is only in your mind.

This is when I will bring up the acronym for fear again, which is False Evidence Appearing Real. Most times, everything we are afraid of comes from little imaginary scenarios happening in our brains. Fear is a direct result of what you're thinking, and it can be controlled (like energy). Remind yourself that you are safe and that you have nothing to be scared of. Have faith in the universe and trust that whatever needs to happen, will happen. Remind yourself that your fears are not going to prevent anything from occurring, but your inner strength and positive dialogue will keep pushing you through anything that comes your way.

3. <u>Understanding that fear comes from our past experiences.</u>

Most of what we fear is something that has happened before and we don't want it to happen again. Or we've seen something happen to others, and we are now afraid of it happening to us. Again, just because we've had a hard experience in our past does not make that true for our future. Unless you would like to continually carry that fear with you, then it will follow you. Those harmful or traumatic experiences that we go through in life are meant to make us stronger, not weaker. Fear is what makes us weaker. So, your goal is to stop reliving the past in fear of it happening again and have strength in knowing it taught you what you needed so that it will never happen again.

4. <u>Repair your psychological outlook and restore your courage.</u>

It's so important for you to change the way your mind looks at things and for you to remember who the hell you are! So instead of thinking, I will never be good enough for that job so I'm not going to try - instead tell yourself: I am worthy, I am confident, and I approve of myself to get this job. After understanding how energy works, it's quite easy to pick up on when your thoughts are attracting fear or courage. When your stomach starts to turn and nausea kicks in (common symptoms of anxiety), remind yourself your fear is creating it, and immediately change to a more positive vibrational energy. Repeat mantras like: I've got this, I can do this, I can be anything I want to be, etc. All kinds of positive affirmations are good for your mental health and to help you find your inner strength and overcome your fears.

5. <u>Send love, not worry.</u>

   I know this was discussed earlier, but it is SO important. Anytime you find yourself getting worried or nervous about a person, situation or outcome, immediately redirect it with a loving energy. For example, if someone is being very cruel to you or causing stress in your life, instead of being worried about what will happen or being angry with them, send love to the situation inside your mind, body and soul. Visualize that person becoming kinder, send them lots of light and prayers to do better. This is especially helpful when dealing with people who are driven by ego or addictions. Being frustrated with them or sending fear their way, will only make the situation and person worse off. Remember that their energy is accepting whatever you are sending them. People who are hardest to love need it more than anything else. Another example would be instead of being worried about getting on an airplane, convince yourself it will be a nice, smooth flight and everything will go by quickly and safely. Basically, it's just vital that when you can feel fear creeping in somewhere in life whether it's about person or event, quickly changing the energy to love instead of fear will only increase your courage and strength allowing you to feel more grounded and at peace.

6. <u>Live in the NOW.</u>

   The final step is to realize that the past cannot affect you and you cannot change the future. So, what you really need to do is... let. it. go.

The only moment we are sincerely in charge of in our lives is what is happening right now. What is happening to you at this moment? Hopefully you are safe, comfortable and reading this book feeling inspired and energized. Focusing on just doing today and constantly keeping yourself in the moment will help cure your depression and ease your anxiety. The only power we really have over our lives is what we choose to do with right now. So, what will you choose? Fear or peace?

According to a course called, 'Releasing Fear through Love' from CIAMSS, it states that "Love is the complete absence of fear." They express that love is divided into two categories, conditional and unconditional. The first, conditional love, comes from the ego. This is love that comes with conditions, such as – I will love you if you do ___. I will love you if you try harder, get sober, get skinnier, or show me more affection, etc. This type of love comes with limitations, whereas unconditional love has none. It is directly from our spirit and involves no part of the ego. That love is constant, and it will proclaim, I love you no matter what!!

One example from my life that was very prominent to show love overcomes fear, was a situation that happened with my father's health. While in the beginning of my metaphysical studies, my dad suffered a heart attack followed by a stroke a few weeks later. This "lifechanging" event hadn't changed him though, not long after it happened, he was still eating unhealthily and choosing poor lifestyle habits. I found myself very angry with him, why wouldn't he change? Why does he want to live that way? It was so frustrating to see him continue to make such poor choices while his health was declining. It was at that time that I began to study the course from CIAMSS, and it really opened my eyes to see I was doing it *all* wrong by reacting this way. Here I was sending the energy of fear to my father, when he needed my love now more than ever. So, I came to the decision that it didn't matter what he ate or what he chose to do with his life, if he were to depart tomorrow, I know that I loved him no matter what. His choices were not mine; they were his. I found out that my fear was coming from not wanting him to leave us and it was really coming from a place of love, but it was my brain that was creating the fear/anger.

It was shortly after I began projecting that different mindset and energy, that my dad began making better choices. I hadn't discussed anything with him, called him or spoken to him. I just changed the way I was looking at the situation and forgave him for all his choices. Then just a few days later, he began riding his bike again daily. He started to change his eating and drinking habits, even letting go of his boat for a kayak instead. I know right?! It sounds exaggerated, but it's not. This is honestly what happened, and from that point on I knew that releasing my fears was going to be the answer to all the struggle and pain I was holding inside.

In my current situations, or my past situations, I had to forgive myself and everyone around me, and let it go. I had no control, and it was more than okay for me to release that. The moment I decided to accept this, my entire life began to change, along with all the people around me. Finally, there was peace in my life, but I had one more vital step to overcome fear, worry, anxiety and depression – and that was to accept and/or offer *forgiveness*.

> For it was when I started to sincerely forgive myself
> and others, that I continued to awaken…

Chapter 4

Forgiveness,
it's for you – not them.

"The act of forgiveness takes place in our mind. It really has nothing to do with the other person."

– Louise Hay

For many, forgiveness is one of life's most difficult challenges. We feel so hurt or betrayed by someone's words or actions; it seems impossible to forgive what they have done. Or it may even be reversed, and you are the one that is yearning for somebody else's forgiveness. There are so many amazing benefits that can come from forgiving yourself or others, including improving your physical and mental health in dramatic ways.

Forgiveness gives us peace of mind and can heal old wounds. It frees us from destructive anger and repairs relationships. Allowing you to feel happier and lighter, improving your overall health. Unforgiveness can lead to a state of chronic anxiety and depression. It can physically make you sick, and if you're fighting major health issues like cancer, it may even delay your healing or recovery process. Most of us don't recognize how much added weight we carry with it until you finally let it go and choose to forgive. If we are upset or mad at someone, it comes from its creator - fear. Every single person in our lives acts as a teacher and if we want others to change, it usually starts by changing *ourselves*. We need to identify our ego and put ourselves in check too.

The word that comes to me now when I think of forgiveness, is courage. It takes a lot of strength to let things go, it's not an easy task. People or situations that hurt so you deeply that the pain and betrayal feel unforgiveable. As I was learning about forgiving, so many powerful quotes came from Bishop TD Jakes. He said, "We think forgiveness is weakness, but it's absolutely not; It takes a very strong person to forgive." His speeches helped me to understand that it is so important to have courage and move forward. Keeping the much-needed faith that what is in front of us, is going to be so much greater than what is behind us. If we don't learn how to forgive from the heart, it's impossible to move forward. You are unable to live and thrive, you will always suffer. If it's constantly in your head making you feel bitter, you're going to carry that with you daily in your life. Bishop Jakes also said, "You cannot embrace your destiny if you do not let go of your history." We all have a history, and I feel confident in believing that not all of it was meant to be moments of pure happiness and joy. As I would love to believe that I now know we are all sent here to learn, and pain is part of that knowledge and growth. Feeling hurt allows us to recognize and appreciate all the good in our life. Forgiving these painful situations is critical to help us release the past and live fully in our present.

It's so important to make the choice, do you want to take on your future and what it has in store? Or do you want to continue to suffer in your history? One of my favorite quotes of all time from Bishop Jakes (told you I learned a lot from his soulful talks) is this: "You have to make a decision. If you want more in the second half of your life, then what you had in the first half of your life, then you're going to have to let the first half go." When I heard him say that I felt it instantly light something up inside of my consciousness. I now understood that when you are always looking backwards, you drain your energy for the "now" – the current moment. You can have a new life, but you need a new mindset to go with it. Holding on to anger and resentment is not going to take you very far. Forgiveness will set you free in ways that you never thought possible. IT'S FOR YOU!

Changing the way you're looking at a situation or person will dramatically change the way you look at forgiveness as well. One thing I started to recognize as I awakened was that many people are the way they are due to the experiences and environments that occurred in their life thus far. Even reminding my own children that those bullies at school who have a difficult time or are cruel to others, must have something bigger going on at home. For if they truly had unconditional love and support in their lives, would they be behaving this way? Maybe they do have love at home, but the energy of their parent's stress is following them to school, so they release it onto others. I feel like that goes for adults as well. What is their life like right now or what was it like growing up? Was it filled with love and compassion, or anger and fear? Forgiving isn't condoning how someone is behaving, what they have done, or even what we have done. It's understanding that we all make mistakes, and we can all change. Every single soul needs forgiveness in their life, even the worst of them. Not because *they* deserve it, but because *you* deserve peace.

In the CIAMSS course 'Releasing Guilt Through Forgiveness' it states that "Forgiveness is the key to freedom from guilt in our lives." It is something we need for ourselves, especially when we carry a lot of regret because of the choices we have made. I found that I had to love myself enough to forgive myself for decisions that I made which caused hurt. Self-love can be extremely hard for many people, almost as hard as forgiveness. What I've learned through all these years of conflict and chaos, is that allowing myself to forgive also allowed me to live again. Feeling so guilty about what I said, what I did or how I made somebody feel would slowly eat me up inside. I cannot even begin to express how incredibly healing it was when I finally let go, and forgave everyone and everything, including myself. To release yourself from that guilt and heaviness upon your shoulders is so freeing and liberating.

Especially if you have the opportunity to apologize to the person that you hurt. Whether it was yourself, or someone else, it creates such a beautiful energy of love and light between you. It rids both of your souls from that destructive anger and resentment. Even if someone does not accept your forgiveness, knowing that you took responsibility for your part is the right thing to do and you should be proud of yourself for doing it. A friendly reminder, karma reacts to genuine energy, so please be sincere and forgive for peace, not righteousness.

I've learned some great ways to help support the road to forgiveness that I like to share with others to help them along their way.

1. <u>Begin to see the benefits for yourself.</u>

Forgiveness is for YOU not THEM; this is a fact. By forgiving you are the one that will reap the benefits. Accepting that you deserve the highest and best in life is very healthy for your mind, body and soul. I could not allow myself to waste any more time or energy on something or someone that can no longer hurt me. When I looked back on the journey with my ex-husband, even though we had some serious toxicity at times, I'm grateful for all that he taught me. There were quite a few things that you would deem unforgivable when it came to our marriage and relationship. Forgiveness included me looking back upon all of it saying, "You know what - thank you! Thank you for being *you* and treating me the way you did. Because of that, you have made ME so much better!" Thinking this way made me feel so much better. I could forgive him because of everything that we went through, it only made me a better version of myself! So, think of it more like, I forgive you because... I'm all good. I'm actually great! What you did taught me a lot, so for that, I forgive you. At this point, I hope you can see and feel how amazing it is when you realize it really is for *you* and not for *them*. This also is the same when forgiving ourselves after we hurt someone else, taking that responsibility and offering our apologies. It has its benefits for them, but it's truly most beneficial for you to heal and move on.

2. <u>Contact the person you need to forgive or be forgiven by. Have open and honest communication, remind yourself, it's just words.</u>

It is amazing how many times I've heard somebody say, "I'm so glad you called I've been meaning to tell you how sorry I was. I was just so concerned that you were so mad at me you wouldn't speak to me." Hearing or speaking those words has the potential to bring immediate relief to someone's soul. Also, knowing when it's your turn to reach out and say, "Please hear me out, I would really like to tell you I'm sorry for how I acted or what I said." It's at that point that we recognize how very significant those words were for that person to hear. I feel like this is such an imperative

41

step when it comes to forgiveness, and even if the person doesn't accept it or refuses to speak to you, walk away knowing that you did your part. Remember, forgiveness – and apologizing – takes courage. Speak your truth.

3. <u>Have empathy for others.</u>

This concept takes us back to what I was discussing earlier in this chapter which is having compassion for what others are going through or have been through. Being an empathetic person means that you're able to sense the emotions of those around you, you literally feel their feelings. This is not always beneficial, so be sure to protect your energy with white light whenever having emotional conversations. Separate in your mind that their feelings are *theirs*, not yours. Having empathy for other people and their situations makes it easier for you to comprehend and forgive. To understand why they are the way that they are and why they make the choices that they make. I've seen many beautiful stories on the internet showing empathy and forgiveness for others. One of them involved a mom shoplifting cereal and milk for her children. Instead of arresting her, the officer offered his forgiveness and understanding to her, and instead decided to purchase the groceries plus more for them. Another one involved a murder trial where a young man was being sentenced for life and he was only 18 years old. The father of the young man that was killed by him, stood in court and offered forgiveness to his son's killer. He had empathy that the young man must have had his own difficult life circumstances that may have greatly influenced his actions and mental state. The father knew they were a huge contribution to his life of violence and crime, and for that he could forgive him. He had compassion for that teenager, and he knew that's what his son would want as well, to forgive him. For all our family and friends in spirit are pure love and light energy that want us to move forward and be at peace. The young man broke down into tears as the two of them embraced and it was probably one of the most beautiful moments I have seen when it comes to offering forgiveness. I can only imagine how proud his son's soul was on the other side of life knowing his dad had the courage to choose peace over anger and resentment.

4. Remember it will take time, so have patience. Forgiveness is a process.

First, I understand that many of you are not going to get done reading this and jump on the phone and start forgiving people or asking for forgiveness. It is definitely a process that we all need to approach when we are ready and willing to truly let go. You must be in all. I also am fully aware that somebody could come from a great loving family and be a wonderful person that just makes extremely poor choices. In that case, we may need to understand that they are still learning how to enlighten and their mistakes along the way will be the karma they need to teach them how to become a better soul. They will just need some time for growth and until that happens, make peace with it, forgive them and move forward. It's not worth waiting around for others to find the light. Whether it's the apology you're waiting for, or their forgiveness, don't let it stop your life

My closing messages on forgiveness include encouraging you to release all the "would of, could of or should of" thoughts in your mind. This is so very important to let go of the "what if" so that the "what is" won't pass you by. Please stop wasting your time and energy on what has happened in your past. Do not let unforgiveness affect the happiness of your destiny and purpose. We have complete control over our energy and how we react. Remembering that how we feel about life and others is what we will attract and having that knowledge will change the way you look at everything.

For it's when I began recognizing that the
energy I was putting out, was exactly what I was
getting back, I continued to awaken...

Chapter 5

It's no lie, it's the
Law of Attraction

*"What you think you become. What you feel you
attract. What you imagine you create."*

– Buddha

At this point, discussing the topics of releasing fears, benefits
of forgiveness, and understanding energy has led us to our next
subject. This is one that I will continue to teach about and preach
about until my time here on Earth has expired. You're probably
familiar with the term 'law of attraction' or maybe the word
'karma', correct? Well to bring you up to speed, here are some
helpful quotes throughout the centuries that refer to the effect of
the law of attraction:

"For as he thinketh in his heart, so is he:"

– Jesus; Proverbs 23:7 KJV

"Energy flows where attention goes."

– James Redfield

"We often become what we believe ourselves to be. If I believe I cannot do something, it makes me incapable of doing it. When I believe I can, I acquire the ability to do it, even if I didn't have it in the first place.

> – Gandhi

"You are the master of your destiny. You can influence, direct, and control your own environment."

> – Napoleon Hill

"If you can dream it, you can do it."

> – Walt Disney

"A person is what he or she thinks about all day long."

> – Ralph Waldo Emerson

"Change your thoughts and you change your world."

> – Norman Vincent Peale

"Think the thought until you believe it, and once you believe it, it is."

> – Abraham Hicks

"The law of attraction states that whatever you focus on, think about, read about and talk about intensely, you're going to attract more of into your life."

> – Jack Canfield

"If you change the way you look at things, the things you look at change."

– Wayne Dyer

"If you think down, you will go down. If you think up, you will go up. You always travel in the direction of your thinking."

– Bishop J.D. Jakes

"What you choose to think about yourself and about life becomes true for you."

– Louise Hay

Honestly, the law of attraction is quite simple; like attracts like, that's all there is to it. If you do good in life, you will get good things. If you do bad things in life, more bad things will come to you. This is why I find it so important to share all these quotes going back to Jesus' era and bringing it forward to modern day motivational speakers. It's not a topic or concept that is new and upcoming on social media. It's something that's been around for thousands of years and taught by many generations. Even Albert Einstein studied quantum physics and the effects of energy for years and said that it does not die, it just changes form. He also said to get what you want in life you must match that 'frequency' of energy to attract it into your life. He knew that everything is made up of energy and that was all there is to know! The sooner you recognize this truth, the sooner you will begin to change how you think, feel and react to life.

So, the main question is: where is your focus right now? Is it on creating the most peaceful existence and environment, or are you focused on the daily drama around you? It's exceedingly important to choose your thoughts and words wisely because you are manifesting them into your reality. Remember that the *energy* you put out is what you get back. You attract what you think and how you feel - it becomes what you are. Knowing this and experiencing it firsthand can make you genuinely careful about what you say and think about a lot.

I had heard of the law of attraction many times before, but never took the topic seriously. It would make my dad and I roll our eyes whenever my mom would try to push it upon us years ago after reading the book "The Secret". My ego was stronger than my spirit back then, it takes lessons and experiences to humble us. Also, whenever I tried to read a book that she would send my way regarding the matter, its vocabulary was way too deep for me. The consciousness of the mind, enlightenment and the chakras were all foreign concepts to me that I wasn't ready to absorb and couldn't comprehend at the time. As I began to grow spiritually in my late twenties and into my thirties, everything really started to make sense! The more you release the ego, the more in tune you become with your spirit and inner self.

Once I began to truly acknowledge and recognize that most of the time, I was thinking the worst, I immediately started to change my thoughts for the better. I discovered that that way of thinking was the root cause of my severe anxiety issues. So, I started to change and embrace the idea that I couldn't fix the past, nor did it have any control of my future. All of it was in my mind and I needed a complete overhaul in the way my brain was functioning. Yeah, I know, I know... easier said than done right? That term, "live in the now" (coined by the spiritual author Eckhart Tolle) was embedded into my everyday life. There was also a daily mantra from the amazing mentor and author Louise Hay, which was "I approve of myself." Both were very influential during my enlightenment journey and helped me learn to how to attract all that I truly desired in my life.

PART 1: LAW OF ATTRACTION: FOR YOURSELF

One thing I genuinely had to understand with the law of attraction was it is not *only* about the positive ways to manifest. We must recognize when we are negatively attracting energy, people or situations into our lives. There are a few ways that we can invite these types of circumstances into our energy. This happens when we are complaining, gossiping, and/or having judgment against others.

Let's start with the daily complaints. Here are a few of my 'favorites' that I have identified over the years, which all of us have said or heard at some point.

1. "My back (or any body part) is always hurting."

Well, saying this *all* the time (even when getting medical help or treatment) means that it will continue to be true. The universe is responding to your words and energy. It does not differentiate between high and low thoughts; it just responds to what it is given. So, continuing to say it hurts or complaining about it will invite the pain to linger. To counter this, try saying "my ___ is healing and feels better each day."

On a spiritual sidenote, as a medium and healer, I have seen that unforgiveness and being stuck in the past means we are holding on to unwanted energy physically in our backs. Remember, it's BEHIND us – the pain, the chaos, the trauma. When you let it go, sincerely and honestly, forgive and move forward – you will begin to see the physical pain go away with it. Same with stress, the weight sits on your shoulders and gets in your neck. Relieve the anxiety, relieve the ache.

2. <u>"It's one thing after another."</u>

Yikes, this one can hit hard if you say it too often, so I always avoid it and tell others to do the same. Please do me a favor and if you find yourself saying this a lot, try your best to stop doing it... like forever and ever my friends! You may get hurt or things can go wrong in your life more frequently for a certain period of time, but that doesn't mean it will stay like that forever. Spiritually, you're just not learning the lessons in what you're going through, so you'll keep attracting them until you do. We need to learn to go through it, and then *go through it*. Take a step back. Observe. Do you talk about how grateful you are for your life and all that it has taught you? Or do you always complain about things going wrong? Taking responsibility for our own negativity is half of the battle. To counteract this one, try saying something like "it is what it is" or "it will always work itself out" and experience it without the stress of trying to change something that cannot be changed. Grow and enlighten from the hard times, it's the best way to utilize the law of attraction for a higher purpose.

3. <u>"I never get to have any fun."</u>

Nope, not with that mindset. Honestly, the only one *choosing* not to have fun – is you! Fear is most likely holding you back. I bet you feel like you can't ask for the time off work or you cannot risk spending the money to go have fun. So, now I ask you - what exactly is 'fun' for you? A vacation? A day of shopping? A day of sleeping? Road trips? It can be whatever you want it to be. Make the time, save up a little money, book the trip or take a mental health day for yourself. Whatever it is, remember that you are in control of the fun in your life. We are only here for so long, so instead of choosing to live life like a robot, allow yourself to have some fun. Counteract this one by saying, "I am inviting more fun, happiness and adventure into my life." Then watch good times just show up in unexpected ways, simply because you said it and believed it.

4. "I can't afford it; I don't have the money."

This is one of the most overstated complaints in life for many people all over the world. The truth may really be that you cannot afford it right now in your current financial circumstances. Or maybe you can pay for it, but there are other priorities in your life, and you don't want to spend the money. That's OK too! You can change your level of wealth, by changing how you think about it. In the course, 'The Principles of Creative Responsibility' from CIAMSS it states "Your prosperity must first be established in your mind... It is vitally important that you accept the responsibility for your prosperity or your lack of prosperity." Making a list of things you want, or desire is a great start to manifesting the wealth to acquire it. Also, positive visualization of seeing your bills fully paid or driving your dream car can also be beneficial in attracting it into reality. Even posting pictures on your refrigerator is a great method to attract the money or things you seek by seeing it, feeling it happening and admiring it often. Finally, one way to keep the money rolling in once it starts is by giving it back out in positive ways. When they ask, "Would you like to round up your total to the nearest dollar to help kids with cancer?" as you go through a fast-food drive-thru, reply "Yes, my pleasure!" Or try donating items to your child's teacher for their class or to a local animal shelter. Paying it forward and doing good deeds for others with our wealth and time will bring it back to you tenfold. For giving is receiving and when it comes from the heart, it's not about the monetary gain, but the spiritual.

It really is as straightforward as it sounds, it's accepting and implementing it that proves to be difficult. I've given you numerous quotes on the law of attraction and multiple examples, but here is the breakdown - whatever you think it will be, it will be. But it doesn't just stop there, you *truly* without ego, must believe it and see it happening for yourself. That is the "secret" to the whole process. You cannot simply just *say* you want something to happen, but you need to really SEE it happening for you. Imagine it clearly in your mind and visualize it as if were happening in real time and do it often. You do not have to figure out all the steps to get there right now, that is where we get stuck. Just see the end result of where you want to be, believe it in your heart and soul to be true, and it will be yours.

So, choose your thoughts and words wisely, because you are manifesting your reality. What you feel is what you are. Begin to use the law of attraction in your favor and visualize/focus/talk about what you WANT. Also, start saying things in a more positive way, that will be vital in giving you a huge energetic boost in the right direction.

Try these sayings:

"It will always work itself out."
"Amazing things happen to me all the time."
"No worries, it is not a big deal."
"I am grateful for this moment."
"I deserve it."

Something I can promise you is that if you start replacing your negative, low energy comments and feelings about life with these types of mantras instead – your life will change dramatically. Guaranteed. It may be difficult to do at first, but once you start doing it, you will never return to your old ways again.

PART 2: LAW OF ATTRACTION:
REGARDING OTHERS

The law of attraction is not only about what thoughts, feelings, words and actions that *you* are putting out into the universe. What type of energy are you taking in from the environment around you? The people that you are near the most have a direct impact on what type of vibe you're attracting and the energies that surround you on a daily basis.

Being around negative people that often complain, are angry or irritable such as spouses, family members, coworkers, etc. will also bring down your energy levels and motivation in life. The ego thrives in your reactions to low vibrations and situations around you such as yelling, crying, judgment, anger, anxiety, revenge, gossip, hatred, prejudice, and depression. These are all examples of how the ego shows itself and things you want to avoid doing in order to attract more positive people and circumstances into your life.

One of the things that I've learned over the years with my education and experiences, may be hard to comprehend at first. This is the fact that others do not _make_ us feel any certain way, we _choose_ how we want to react to them. They may be acting or doing something that encourages you to reply in anger or ego, but getting ahead of it is a practice that takes time. It is so hard to do – to not react. But when you start to see that *you* are the one accepting what's being given to you from others, you start to choose who you surround yourself with much more carefully. Knowing your boundaries is key in showing the universe what type of people are welcomed into your precious energy.

You can help boost the vibrations of those you attract around you, first make sure you are very clear to the universe about who you will accept into your circle. Always ask for the highest and best in family, friends and others around you such as coworkers or clients. Keep the positive vibes going out by truly wanting and wishing the best for all souls that you come across. The ones that are hardest to love are the ones that need it more than anything else, because they have none for themselves. Give compliments often to those you love or random people you come across, it's like verbal sunshine and makes you feel good too.

Remember, in most circumstances it is your free will and self-choice of whom you want to share your energy with on a normal basis. Remove toxic energy from your inner circle and watch yourself begin to thrive without that added weight holding you down. It doesn't matter if they are immediate family, best friends from childhood, or someone we still truly love. When you're no longer feeling unconditional love from them, you can be grateful for the time spent together and the lessons learned along the way. Then, let them go. There is no physical or spiritual law that states we must continue sharing our lives with someone regardless of how they treat us, biologically connected or not.

Personal boundaries are healthy and necessary, no matter what the relationship is.

PART 3: LAW OF ATTRACTION: LOVE

Now this is where I wish I would have known about the law of attraction sooner! Love can be so overwhelming, especially for empathetic souls. Have you ever been so drawn to another person, that no matter how badly they hurt you, you still pursue them? Well, now I know that "attraction" always tends to have a higher purpose or lesson attached to it. Whether it be for you, for them or both of you.

You attract people into your life that have the same energy vibration as you do at that time in your life. Just like we discussed energy in the beginning of this book, it is recognized like the pull of a magnet by those around you. Like attracts like. Two souls with low energy (depression, anxiety, heartbreak, etc.) colliding may *seem* to need each other in the moment, but truly they both need healed individually first. If both are trying to repair their hearts at the same time they're trying to love another, they will become frequently imbalanced with each other's energy. When one of you is up and the other one is down, they may bring you down too. Remember you absorb each other's energy so trying to pick yourself up while trying to pick up another person at the same time, is simply too much weight to bear. This creates triggers and cycles that are unhealthy and ultimately may lead to the demise of the relationship.

It's much healthier to seek out or manifest love and relationships when you're feeling happy, confident, grounded and secure. Now *that* is the type of energy that you want to be matched with and attracted to. Two high energy souls who are fully healed will be able to recover and cope much easier when conflict arises. They will have the capability mentally and emotionally to keep each other going and motivated. Understanding and respecting one another's healthy boundaries along with positive communication will allow both of you to thrive. This is the type of energy to attract genuine, unconditional love into your life!

Remember, what we say and feel about relationships is what you are going to attract (just like money). When I hear people saying things like: "I always find narcissists to date" or "I have terrible luck in relationships", I immediately want to tell them to stop saying those things! If you truly believe that you will only attract someone in a connection that will hurt you, or bring you down, then that is exactly what you will end up getting. Narcissists love to prey upon on the emotionally weak and tired. Sensitive souls with low self-esteem that don't think much of themselves is dangerous territory. They will swoop in and seem like the best thing that could have happened to you. Coming across confident and ready to love and fix you, seemingly beginning to put you back together. Feels REALLY good at first, because their ego is being fueled with a superior level of importance for being your savior. Truly it is not about being happy they are helping you, it's how it is making *them* feel that is boosting their energy.

It is when that moment finally comes that you begin to feel good about yourself again, that they will instantly change. Insulting you and putting you down to a lower level so that you may never rise above theirs. The better you get, the worse they become because they always want you beneath them. I ask that you please do yourself a favor and start genuinely loving yourself. Every moment of every day. So much that you have the power and ability to reject narcissism in any type of relationship in your life, romantic or personal. It doesn't matter who they are, you always deserve to be treated with respect and love from those around you.

When you truly begin to increase your self-worth, self-confidence and self-love, you begin to attract the highest and best love from another. Again, saying positive affirmations and mantras to yourself in replacement of negative thoughts or experiences, will be life changing for you. What you want to say out loud as well as internally, are uplifting words and descriptions of what you would like in a romantic partner. Tell the universe exactly what you want in a soulmate and be sure to believe that you deserve it! That's the most important part about the law of attraction in general, is believing it and trusting it will manifest.

For myself, I would say things such as "I am attracting a grounded, mature, sober, spiritual, motivated, kind, funny and loving romantic companion in my life. I appreciate the love lessons of my past, and I now know what is best for me. I recognize what I deserve, and I will accept nothing less. My partner will make me always feel safe in their presence and I can be my true authentic self with this person. I know they will come to me when the time is right, and I will appreciate the pause while I wait for them to come into my energy and life." Now saying *this* is a much more effective way of attracting who I want to love and be loved by. Shine that inner light so bright it attracts the highest love and blinds the rest from ever seeing you in the first place.

PART 4: LAW OF ATTRACTION: MONEY

We touched on this topic earlier in the chapter when discussing the law of attraction for yourself and watching the words we say. I stated that how you view money and your personal relationship with it will directly affect how you are going to attract it in your life. Reminding you once again, that what you think, feel and say is what you are going to experience. The most successful people in the world understand the law of attraction and how vital it is to have a positive mindset on money. Those that believe they will always remain at a certain level in life, especially in regard to their career and finances, will stay at that level.

Seeing yourself being extremely wealthy and successful will only help push you there faster. It's not just as easy as thinking and feeling it though, you must start there and then put in the work to get the momentum flowing. As a great mentor of mine, the late Rev. John White from Lilydale once told me, "Sincerity is key in attracting what we want." So, when you tell yourself, I'm going to be a successful and abundant _____ (doctor, artist, entrepreneur, CEO, athlete, etc.) in an honest and sincere energy, you will give yourself the momentum needed to achieve it. When you are always sincere in your actions and words, it will increase the momentum of attraction in your life.

Telling yourself the opposite such as: I'm not good enough, well trained enough, can't afford school, I have no talent or skill, etc. will hinder your progress dramatically, if not completely. Turning "I can't" into "I can" is such a game changer in life when it comes to one's success. Like my example earlier on fear, Mohammad Ali said "I am the greatest", because he truly believed he was and led a successful career in boxing. This doesn't just apply to your career or job choices, but to your relationship with money in general. Constantly complaining about your financial situation or saying low energy comments like "I could never afford that" or "I will be in debt forever" will only continue to impede monetary success in your life. Remember, words said internally or externally carry energy with them, so choose yours carefully when it comes to money and finances.

PART 5: LAW OF ATTRACTION:
MY REAL-LIFE EXPERIENCES

The personal stories I'm about to share with you from my real-life experiences involving the law of attraction are truthful and honest. Some of them even occurred before I began studying the topic or understanding what it was all about. I'm now able to look back upon my life and see how I was receiving exactly what I was giving in to the universe. I will begin with the most profound life changing experience for me to date, that will only prove and validate the power of the law of attraction.

In the year 2012, I had become the most overweight and unhappy version of myself. I was ready to end my marriage and had very little self-confidence or hope for the future. At the time, I still had over $50,000 to pay off in student loans that helped me earn my degree in early childhood education. The monthly payments were at five-hundred dollars a month, which was about half of each paycheck I received as a second-grade teacher. In my mind and in my heart, I knew there was no way I was getting out of this marriage or terrible situation unless I somehow got rid of this huge debt. I knew that if I could alleviate that massive weight which was holding me back, I would finally find my freedom and myself again.

So, I began to focus on what I could possibly do to earn that much money and get it quickly. I thought to myself, how does somebody get a large abundance of money like that immediately and all at once? I guessed they would have to win it by entering a contest, selling their items or winning the lottery. Suddenly, it hit me! I could go be on a game show! I had been acting and doing theater since I was a child, along with dance classes and the whole nine yards. I loved being on stage or in front of a camera so that part was easy for me. It was finding the right type of show that

I knew I would be successful on so that I could help myself out financially as much as possible.

Now being a medium at this point in my life, I look back and realize that all of these "a-ha moments" were in fact messages from spirit coming in very quickly. I would rarely have the capability of thinking this type of solution up so rapidly, I now know that it was my loved ones in spirit helping push me in the right direction. They provided me with the guidance I needed to attract financial freedom and happiness into my life. It was then that I suddenly had a flashback to when I was just a child and we lived with my mother's father, aka 'Papa' and he loved to watch the gameshow, Wheel of Fortune. He always told me I was going to be Vanna White one day while we would sit together and watch the show. It was a lot of fun for us, and I enjoyed the race of trying to solve the phrases before he did. As soon as I recalled that memory, I searched for the Wheel of Fortune's website and found the application to be a contestant on the show.

When I began to fill it out, it asked a few random questions that I assumed would only help boost my chances of being on the show. A few that stuck out to me which I could answer 'yes' to were, "Are you a teacher?" and "Are you or someone in your family serving active duty in the military?". After submitting the application, it took a few weeks, but then it came. I received an e-mail inviting me to audition for the show!! My energy and excitement went through the roof when I received that message. I felt like I was in a dream, but reminded myself I didn't make it on there yet. There was work to be done! The audition would be three hours away from where I was living at the time on the other coast of Florida, but it was of no concern to me. Without hesitation, I made the drive and even took my older brother with me as a good luck charm and cheerleader.

During the audition, I remember that the entire time I kept an

"I can do this" energy and had found my confidence in my ability to 'act' like a great game show contestant. I made sure that I caught eyes with the producers who were watching, maintained a great smile and attitude. All those years of being on stage and in front of the camera were paying off. It wasn't just about being a good contestant but also about putting on a good show!

After the first few rounds, they announced that they would only be keeping twenty of us for the final part of the audition. If we didn't hear our name called, better luck next time and thank you for coming out. As they began reading the names, I kept thinking to myself "they are going to call my name". (You can picture me almost passing out from holding my breath as they read each name aloud ha-ha!) I just so happened to be the *second to last* name that they called on the list! Once again, the outside of me seemed in control, but inside my energy was the highest it had ever been in my life. I continued to give it my best through the remainder of the audition and shine in the moment like I was really on the show. I was feeling extremely grateful to have made it that far and to have had the experience in general.

When we finished, the producers thanked us again and let us know that we would receive a letter within exactly 14 days if we had made it onto the show. If we didn't receive that letter, best of luck next time. They reiterated that it would not arrive any later than that so folks wouldn't hold out false hope for too long. The next two weeks of my life felt like one hundred years! After the 14th day passed my heart dropped and I thought how can this be? I *really* believed in my heart and soul that I made it! Well, the universe likes to be humorous sometimes, so my casting letter to be on Wheel of Fortune came on the 15th day.

That burst of excitement returned to me instantly, I felt my energy lift and my happiness soared above the clouds. It was like having an out of body experience when I knew I was going to be on

Wheel of Fortune!! It was from that point forward that no matter what happened, my mind was set on winning. I knew this was a blessing and I could be leaving with money from the show to help me pay for my student loans and get a much-needed divorce. My goal and dream of being on the show was sincere. It would not only be an amazing once in a lifetime opportunity, but the solution that could finally help me rebuild and restart my life. I knew that win or lose, I was going to give it my all, all the way till the end.

As many are unaware of the process, it would not be instant but rather take six months before I got the phone call that I would be taping in late October of 2012. I had just started a new teaching position at a charter school, so when I received the news, I had to let my boss know I would be needing some time off at some point in the year to be on the show. The look on his face said it all! He was completely thrilled for me and in full support of my journey. (Sidenote: This is a direct example of the law of attraction with others, the support from my job was vital in helping to boost my positive energy.) The community of the school rallied behind me and their excitement for my opportunity only propelled me higher in that beautiful vibe I was feeling at the time. You can imagine there was at least one person who wasn't so happy with my success, but nothing was getting me down at that point. The light was starting to shine brightly at the end of the dark tunnel that surrounded me, and I couldn't get to it soon enough.

When it was time for me to choose a guest to come with me to the show, it didn't take long for me to decide that it had to be my mom. She had been my rock my entire life and there was no way I was going through this experience without her. If anyone would encourage me and motivate me to be a winner, it was my mother. I know that her enthusiasm and upbeat energy was exactly what I needed to get the most out of this opportunity. My dad was also a huge support, and I was able to leave my toddler daughter back home knowing she was in his loving care. Now looking back at it, this just reiterates the need to only surround yourself with people who build you up, support you and cheer you on to achieve your highest dreams and ambitions. The positive energy you give to yourself in life is so important, so is who you receive it from.

What I didn't understand then that I completely do now, was that my *entire* experience was manifested by the law of attraction. I had done everything right to get to that moment. There was a genuine need for money, I believed I could do well on the show, and I could visualize myself winning. Then, bam! It was happening, I was on my way to Culver City Studios in California and to the production set of a world-renowned game show. There was nothing in that moment that could get me down. No matter what happened, I was so thankful to be where I was and absorbing every single moment of it. Now some would want to say it was all "luck" or my previous experience/training in acting that was what helped boost my odds of being on the show. Which I'm sure it did! But I also know with 100% certainty that *my* energy, *my* thoughts and *my* actions were extremely significant in creating this amazing moment in my life.

During the entire process from start to finish, I kept myself pumped up and motivated. I was thrilled and so very ready to fully embrace this once-in-a-lifetime opportunity that I was presented with. I earned my way there and I now know that I manifested it by staying positive from the very beginning. I was truly genuine in my purpose and sincere in what I needed to happen. I wanted to pay off that 50K in student loans, which was the whole reason I even went on the show. I kept telling myself subconsciously – "I'm going to win; I can do this!" I even made sure to wish the other two contestants that were on the episode with me good luck before we went out, because I knew that all of us had an opportunity to win some money. So how great would that be if we could all succeed and go home with some winnings? Awesome, right?! Again, now looking back at it, I realize those acts of genuine kindness were just another checkmark on my positive karma list. Every single thing I did or said was continually feeding the momentum towards one of the greatest moments of my life.

The mediumship side of my experience will be discussed in a later book, but the human side of my experience is what I will continue to talk about leading up to the conclusion of the show. For clarification, I had not been professionally practicing or developing as a psychic medium until a few years after the show was aired. I had known about the abilities of loved ones in my family since I was a child, but at this time I was degreed in early childhood education and teaching elementary students. Another check on that positive karma list, I told my class that if I won enough money on the show, I would take them all to Chuck E' Cheese. The charter school I taught at was specifically created to aid and be sanctuary to the most poverty-stricken children of the local area. A class trip to an arcade was a major treat for them and a special gift that would fill their hearts with so much joy. Well, spoiler alert... I was able to fulfill that promise to my students!

Keeping a big smile on my face and thankfulness in my heart, I became one of the champions of Wheel of Fortune. In the end, I won enough money to pay for my flight and trip out to California, as well as pay the required taxes from my winnings. I also solved the puzzle needed to win an all-expense paid trip to an exclusive resort in Saint Lucia. As some would say, I cleaned up! The final puzzle answer quite literally popped out of my mouth and when I realized I had won the show, all I wanted to do was hug my mom! The host at the time, Pat Sajak, asked me if I wanted to see what I had won, and when he flipped open my prize... it read $50,000. The *exact amount* I needed to pay off my student loans and start the next chapter of my life. The entire reason I was there. As my mom ran out to greet me on stage, the first thing she said to me was, "Now you can pay off your student loans!" We cried and hugged with joyful tears of happiness as my mother, my best friend and biggest fan, was there to share in one of the most exhilarating moments of my lifetime.

So, now when you hear the saying, you can do anything you put your mind to, please believe it. This experience proved to me that what we put out into the universe is exactly what we are going to get back. I know with certainty if my mindset was more in that of fear or ego when I went on the show, I would have never made it as far as I did. Any moments of greed or selfishness would quite definitely have led to a different outcome. But I stayed excited, grateful and positive the entire time. I *saw* myself winning and I *knew* I could do it. That was exactly what was needed from my energy to attract the success that I did. Life after the show only continued to prove to me that if I just planted the seed of what I desired into the universe, it would help me to do anything I put my mind to.

By 2018, I had become certified as an intuitive medium, ordained as a spiritualist minister and had started my own business. We had been transferred from Florida to Buffalo, NY and we were able to begin the separation process after twenty years together. The money from the show paid off my loans and the equity from the sale of our Florida home gave me the flexibility I needed to finally pursue a divorce. (Another example of how things will work themselves out once you believe!) We were renting a home outside of Buffalo at the time, and I knew when the school year ended, it would be the opportunity we needed to move into our own separate residences. The search for a new place began in February, and yes looking for a home in Buffalo in the middle of winter is quite the task when there is twelve inches of snow! Yet the weather did not hinder us, and we made it to an open house for a beautiful home in a great neighborhood near an elementary school.

There had to be at least 20 people in the home aside from us, everyone seemingly loving the house as they walked through it. The only issue we had in making an offer was that we couldn't get out of our lease from the rental home until July 1st and that was the soonest that we could move. How would it be possible with all these other people who were probably ready to buy now? It seemed like our chances were going to be slim to none. On our way out, we met the realtor who was selling the home for the owners and let her know how interested we were in the home. She said thank you so much, adding that if we had an offer to try to send it to her by that evening as they were expecting quite a few. It was then that she also let us know there was only one major contingency, they can't move out until July as they're waiting for their new home to be built. In my mind, I was FREAKING out!! We excitedly replied that that would be perfect for us because we were in the same situation. Of course, when we put in our offer that evening, it was accepted! Finally, I was about to have freedom for the first time in twenty years and it was like the universe was just opening the door for me and said welcome home! Your new future looks bright, and you deserve it!

Over a year later in the summer of 2019, I began feeling like maybe next year it would be best to consider moving again. This time to go back to my hometown in Ohio where my ex-husband and I were both born and raised. The kids needed stability, especially my oldest child, because they had been moved all over the east coast due to their father being in the military. My son was going to kindergarten that following year and my daughter was beginning her first year in middle school. Plus, after that year their dad would be transferred again, which meant yet another move for them regardless.

I began talking about another possible move with my family and friends to get their input and I was relaxed when we spoke because I had the time to think about it before deciding. There was no rush and I still had until the next year to make my final choice. So, I continually kept saying "I will know by March. Spirit will show me the way. I will know what to do by March." I said this over and over for months whenever anyone asked if I was still moving home. Fall and winter came and went when out of nowhere around late February, my neighbor messaged me and asked, "Hey, are you still thinking about selling the house and moving back to Ohio? I have a buddy who really wants to move into this neighborhood, and when I told him that you may move, he said he would offer you asking price. He just wanted to take a look at the home with his girlfriend first, but he was serious. He really wants your house." I was in complete shock reading his text and quite astonished to have received it when I did! I was talking about it a lot more back in the summer and fall, but life continued and it went to the back burner in my brain momentarily. I did not even have it listed on the market, I just said "Sure! How about on Friday? They can come look and although it isn't listed yet, I am not opposed to discussions ahead of time!" They agreed and the couple came to see the house (the first week of March) and fell in love with it. They offered me full price, without any contingencies on their end. It was like I was in a dream yet again, did that just work itself out THAT well?

If that wasn't enough of a sign, that night I prayed and asked the universe to show me more validation that it was time to move back home to Ohio. The next morning, I got in my car to take my son to school, and the radio was playing a commercial. Instantly, I hear "Are you ready to sell your home? Our Realty Group is ready to help you!!" Again... I was in amazement. I smiled and laughed knowing it was the universe and my angels telling me it was time, time to go home. We agreed to sell and right as the process began with contracts, etc. COVID-19 hit the world, shutting down quite literally everything and everyone. Yet once again it just so happened that the timing would work out perfectly so that the sale wasn't hindered at all. The couple that was moving in was flexible with their time, which was so helpful for us to find a home in Ohio and not feel rushed. Plus, everything was closed so there was no way to start the process again until places reopened. This gave the children time to finish the school year out at home and by the summer we could move. The timing was wild, but it worked out perfectly. Everything happened exactly as it needed to even during the chaos of COVID. My divorce was about to be finalized and life kept sending me signs to reassure me that I was right where I needed to be. I earned it!

At first thought, it seemed as though it was going to be more difficult to afford a big enough home for me and the children on my now single mom salary. While the pandemic was such a devastating time for so many, there was some light in it for us as the interest rates on homes had taken a major plunge due to the shutdown. This may not have worked out well for the banks and housing industry, but at the time it made it much easier for folks like me. We had the opportunity to acquire a home that would be just the right size for us and affordable. As we began the search, it was a snail's pace as there were not many homes to view since the market was *just* opening back up. I felt myself start to panic and become stressed that it may take longer than I thought. Recognizing the thoughts were coming from a place of fear, I instantly changed them to everything was working out as it should. Trust and have faith in the universe that the perfect house would come at just the right time. It has worked out thus far and it will continue to by keeping a positive mindset.

Finally, once I relaxed and resumed a better outlook, a home came around that seemed to be a great fit for us. There were a few things that I would have wanted differently in regards the house, but I was ready to just settle for what I could get and take the positives over the negatives to get us settled and moved back home. There were a few points that we were asking of the owner which the realtor assured us they would do if we locked in a contract. Well, once we wrote up an offer, we heard back from the homeowner, and he refused to make any of the changes we were asking for. I was devastated, it seemed like it was going to work out and it was where we were going to be moving in. Once again before the anxiety could kick in, I took a deep breath and assured myself it just wasn't the house. They didn't want me to settle and what I didn't know at that moment was how grateful I was about to be that that home did not work out! Spirit had a better plan for us with a home that would be the absolute perfect place to start this new chapter in our lives.

A few more weeks went by, and I was trying to continually keep the faith and trust that the right home would come soon. The funny thing about spirit, is they are always in time and on time, but most of the time, it's not when we want it to be! It's typically just in the nick of time that everything tends to work itself out in the best of ways. This was exactly how our ideal home would present itself, right when we really needed it to. I was calm in my energy and had just sat down for my coffee after taking in the beautiful morning sun. I jumped online to see if there were any updates or new homes on the market. It had been days since anything new was listed, and as soon as I got on the site, I saw the house and intuitively knew it was going to be ours. It had only been listed for an hour so I called my realtor as quickly as I could with excitement and told her to put an offer on the home contingent upon me seeing it. I would have to make that 3-hour drive the next day to look at it in person, but I already knew, it was the one.

When we arrived, the house had been sitting vacant for about nine months. So, it definitely needed some love, but the entire property was my dream. The front porch swing and the huge, beautiful backyard that went into trees and privacy was in my vision of what I wanted in a home. Not to mention the amazingly beautiful weeping willow that I instantly fell in love with. A swimming pool for the kids complete with a sundeck for mom and a big country home with large bedrooms. It was perfection. The owner was incredibly kind and easy to work with, and although the closing date moved around more than we would have liked, again it just happened to be great timing for our transition back home. Everything was working out and I couldn't have been happier or more motivated to start over.

Now the last example of real-life law of attraction moments in my life happened after we moved in July of 2020. My parents had come up from Florida to help me get situated into the new home. My dad loves to do everything he can for my children to fully enjoy their childhood. So, he decided to build them a treehouse in our backyard like he did for my brothers and I when we were kids. After it was built, my friend and I were discussing how a sliding board coming down the side of it would be the perfect addition. We were about to start the hunt for one that week, when a few days later my new neighbor texted me. (Now an important part to mention is that I had just met these folks a few times at this point, and we had never discussed the situation with the treehouse.) She ends up, out of NOWHERE, sending me a picture of this large, green sliding board from a play set and said, "Hello! We have this solo green sliding board that we were about to get rid of and thought it would make a great addition to your new treehouse. Would you like to have it?" Mind. Blown. I think my jaw literally hit the floor when I got this text message. I had *just* told my father about it as well and almost instantly it was right in front of me! I would say it was quite unbelievable, but the way life was going for me at that point – this was par for the course.

As we settled into our new home and new life, I reflected on all the situations and circumstances that had to happen exactly the way they did to get us there. It was from that point on that I accepted and went along with all the ups and downs in my life. From my experiences, I have learned to quite literally 'go with the flow' and have an 'attitude of gratitude' with all that life hands you. Keeping a positive outlook on life and knowing I can do anything I put my mind to is something I will continue to do for the rest of my days. For I know with certainty now, that whatever I put my energy towards, I will receive.

As I conclude this chapter, I just want you to look back at your own life and recognize how the law of attraction has worked for you and against you thus far. Are you able to identify those times where your emotional mindset was of a lower vibrational energy and your words were unhealthy towards yourself or others? Do you recall how those times made you feel mentally and physically? Can you remember the times you were most successful in your life? Was it also the times that you had the most confidence in yourself and great support from those around you? Or maybe it was the time when you had no support, so you gave it your all and supported yourself to become successful without anyone else's help. No matter what you answer to any of these questions, it will become more evidential as you look back upon your journey. You will start to see the highs and lows of your path here in life were a direct result of yourself and the energy surrounding you at the time. Now that you understand the power of manifesting, choose to live positively in the moment and remember to go with the flow one day, one moment, at a time.

For it was in those few moments a day when I would
stop to breathe and be at peace in the moment of
now, that I continued to thrive and awaken…

71

Laura Lynn on Wheel of Fortune (Dec. 11, 2012)

Chapter 6

Meditation is
Medication for the Soul

"The gift of learning to meditate is the greatest
gift you can give yourself in this lifetime."

– Sogyal Rinpoche

The first time I tried meditation or even heard about it was when I was eleven years old visiting our cousin, the psychic medium, in Arkansas. Mary Linn tried her best to teach me the process, but at that age I had anything *but* patience. I tried to relax and breathe as she instructed my mom and I as we sat at the darkened dining room table in her home. I remember it being difficult for me to sit still and keep my eyes closed for a longer of a period of time. Meditation seemed kind of silly to me back then, like what was the point of just sitting here and breathing? As I closed my eyes and focused on the darkness I continued to breathe deeply. Soon, I felt like I was in a whole other world, my entire body was relaxed, and my forehead felt tingly. It felt as though I was dreaming but while awake. Looking back, I wish I would have continued to meditate after we returned home. It would have helped reduce my anxiety dramatically as a child, but I had to go through that part of my journey for growth. This first experience was a great introduction to how it was done and truly opened me up to the process more as an adult.

Almost twenty years later in 2013, Mary Linn returned to my life on a full-time basis when she and her husband Thomas moved only a few miles down the street from me in Florida. After her arrival, was when she let me know that I should begin to develop as a medium and learn how to meditate with her. I almost laughed at her when she said that and exclaimed "I can't meditate! I can't sit still for that long!" To which she replied, "Well, then, that means you need it even more!" She was right, I needed a way to disconnect from the chaos of everyday life and find a few moments of peace. I was still on cloud nine from my Wheel of Fortune win the previous year, but reality and normal life would kick back in along with my depression.

As I recalled, I did enjoy that meditation when I was younger, even though it was hard for me to do at first. I felt as though being an adult it may prove to be *more* difficult with having so many things on my mind at one time. In the end, I decided to try it and gave it another chance. I began taking classes with Mary Linn and participating in her weekly meditation groups. When I say it changed my life, that is not an understatement. As the quote that opens this chapter says, it is the greatest gift I ever gave myself and that she ever gave to me. Learning how to meditate has made a dramatic difference in balancing my mind, body and soul. It was like anything else we tried for the first time, once you get into the groove and figure it out, it becomes much easier to do. Initially, you begin to get used to the process and make it your own by finding what type of meditation style works best for you. That will help you figure out how to get the most out of your meditations.

Our spirit is pure energy that is made up of love and light.

Our inner self is that part of us that always leads our thoughts and feelings to the highest and best in our life. It's always been there but can get lost in life and the development of the ego. We usually find it again when we are faced with life's most difficult challenges. That voice in your head that always guides you to do what's right is your inner voice. That "other" more negative voice is the ego and it's important to know the difference. Our thoughts can create fear, where intuition will always guide you to a place of positivity and love. We need to realize that the answers we seek can only be found using our inner guide, not from the outside world around us. That our environment can influence us, but our intuition channels us to do what we truly need. So, how do we find that positive and helpful inner voice? You guessed it, meditation!

Now most of the time when I mention using meditation as medication to people, they reply in a similar way that I did – which was "Oh I cannot meditate! I don't know how to turn my mind off." So of course, it's only normal for me to reply the way she would want me to – "That is perfect, that means you need it even more!" It's really about being able to release yourself from the busy ever moving hamster wheel of daily life by jumping off it. Turning off all the noise from life to be in moment of stillness, solitude and quiet. It's here that we find ourselves, our *true* self – the spirit.

Listed below are some great tools that you can use to help you get started on making meditation part of your daily routine. I promise once you find your inner peace, you'll be eager to revisit and maintain it as often as possible.

1. The number one focus with meditation is your <u>breathing</u>.

    Breathwork and learning how to control it is vital for you to have a successful meditation. Have you ever been told when you are panicking to slow down and take a deep breath? Focusing on big, deep breaths in and out instantly relaxes the mind and body. I found that counting while I was doing my breathwork was very helpful when I began learning how to meditate. Try counting using the method 4-4-4. Breathe in for four seconds, hold your breath for four seconds, then release for four seconds. You can increase or decrease the number of seconds depending on your level of comfortability. Using this method will help your focus remain strictly on your breathing and not allow interference from other pesky (normal) distracting thoughts.

2. The next important part of meditation is <u>creating your own "Zen" space</u>.

    This will be a spot where you can feel completely comfortable and relaxed. Some people prefer to sit in a crisscross position with their hands on their knees. I prefer to sit in a comfortable chair, upright with my feet flat on the floor and my palms facing upward in my lap. One of my favorite places to meditate is outdoors where I can listen to the natural sounds of Mother Nature like birds, water and wind. Either way, find your space and make sure the energy is peaceful and calm. I love to light scented candles, burn incense or use an essential oil diffuser to create a beautiful aromatherapy that I personally enjoy. The more comfortable you are, the better the meditation will be!

3. The next important choice with your meditation is your <u>audio</u> selection.

    This can be a very valuable tool to use during meditation. You also want to do a little research and listen to the meditation music or guided meditation *all the way through* before you try it. We all have different tastes in relaxing music and how we enjoy the sound of someone's voice. I will never forget when I was completely relaxed after one of my first meditations with music on YouTube, and a commercial came on instantly when the music ended. I had my headphones on full blast with the volume up so I would feel completely engulfed in the experience of meditation. Ha - I about jumped out of my comfy chair when that ad came on, it was quite startling! More lessons learned and I have found it very important to familiarize yourself with what you're listening to first, so you're prepared. You can also pay for or download certain meditation-based apps to exclude any type of commercial interruption. Finally, as I stated earlier, another option for audio with your meditation is to be outside in nature or to listen to nature sounds. Some people find comfort in hearing thunderstorms, the singing of birds, trickling creeks or the waves by the ocean. Whatever it may be, peaceful nature sounds can be a beautiful, relaxing choice when it comes to our sound environment during meditation.

4. For me, <u>aromatherapy</u> is a huge part of my daily meditation and something I prefer to have whenever I'm meditating or for relaxation. Just like music or sounds, what we enjoy as far as smells is distinct for everybody. You may not be an incense person and only enjoy candles. If you're looking for a more holistic and healing approach to aromatherapy, I highly encourage you to try natural essential oils. It is important when choosing oils, to verify they are genuine. Like sounds, do your research and see which brand and scent best fits your needs. It's important to know the product you are getting because inhaling non-organic

substances into your lung's during meditation is not going to be beneficial. The incense, candles or oils that you use should have a scent that is pleasing and relaxing to you, but also healthy. For example, peppermint/lavender combinations of essential oils can create a calmer aroma whereas lemon/citrus blends may increase one's energy.

5. Then there is <u>the timing of the session</u>.

How long should you meditate for? This varies for everyone and is dependent upon your availability and flexibility when it comes to scheduling your meditation times. Sometimes you may find yourself just closing your eyes to take a deep breath for a few moments of meditation while you're at a stoplight or at work in the middle of your busy day. You may feel more comfortable in a 10- or 15-minute meditation knowing it's just long enough to give you that inner peace for your day without taking up too much time. Some prefer a longer meditation or to use meditation during a time of day when it's most beneficial for them. It is suggested that you try meditation when you first wake up in the morning feeling that hazy energy before you begin your day. Or in the evening, when you are ready to relax and get some peaceful rest. It is my recommendation that you do not meditate more than twenty to thirty minutes at a time when not utilizing it for sleep. The purpose of meditation is to be aware of that feeling of relaxation and inner peace, and not to fall asleep! So, if that is something that you do easily once you close your eyes, make sure you're in an upright position and try shorter or open eye meditations (staring at a flame, object or scenery).

6. Finally, there are a few <u>different types of meditation</u> that you may choose from to find the one most beneficial to you.

Some examples include:

a. <u>Breath Awareness Meditation</u> - this is a more basic and common method of meditating which consists of finding that comfortable Zen spot we discussed earlier, closing your eyes and putting all your attention on the inhaling and exhaling of your breath.

b. <u>Mindfulness Meditation</u> - this form of meditating encourages you to remain aware and present in the current moment. Again, focusing on your breathing or an object to improve the awareness of yourself and the environment around you. When your mind begins to wander, you simply acknowledge it and return to your focus. Similar to breathwork, this is one of the most popular forms of meditation.

c. <u>Guided Meditation</u> - this type of meditation is instructed vocally by another person. Whether it be a live group meditation or through an instructional video or app, many websites have free guided meditations to get you started. Reminder to do your research and find an instructor with a voice that is satisfying and tolerable during your meditation. Many times, beginners find it helpful to use this type of meditation as they begin to explore what works for them.

d. <u>Movement Meditation</u> - this can also be beneficial for beginners or as an introduction to meditation for the 'busy bodies.' Acknowledging that it can be hard to sit still for several minutes, this type of meditation may be most useful for those that enjoy movement for focus. Some common practices of this type of meditation include Tai chi, yoga or Qi gong.

e. <u>Transcendental or Mantra Meditation</u> - the goal of this type of meditation is to repeat a mantra or word in your mind and focus on that during your session. Repeating phrases helps maintain focus and allows us to deepen our awareness. This is a prominent form of meditation in Hindu and Buddhist traditions. Using a repetitive sound to clear the mind is also a great alternative for people who don't enjoy silence. Some enjoy this type of meditation because they find it easier to focus on a word or phrase rather than on their breath. You may repeat the mantras inwardly and silently choosing peaceful words such as 'ohm' or 'breathe'. Or by choosing longer mantras to focus on such as "I feel at peace" or "I am grounded".

f. <u>Visualization Meditation</u> - this type of meditation is a technique focused on imagining positive scenes, visions or situations occurring in your life. It is important to try and utilize your inner awareness in this visualization to add as much detail as possible. Use all five senses while imagining yourself succeeding at specific goals, accomplishments and dreams. Many will use this type of meditation to help manifest what they are visualizing into their reality. It is a great source to get you where you want to be faster in life!

Over time and through trial and error, you will find the meditation method, sounds, scents and environment that works best for you. While exploring different types of meditations, take note of which of them leave you feeling most relaxed, at peace and clear minded. Then you can decide which type of meditation is most beneficial for you personally and create that Zen environment for yourself at home to practice in.

BENEFITS OF MEDITATION – PHYSICALLY AND EMOTIONALLY

There is a reason that meditation is the most widely used practice amongst the more successful people in the world. It is such a powerful method to use in order to reduce stress, calm the mind and create a sense of balance in your internal and external worlds. The advantages of meditation are endless in the ways that it can help us physically, mentally, emotionally and spiritually.

Mentally, meditation will improve your focus, creativity and clarity. It will assist in dramatically reducing your anxiety levels. It will help you to manage any type of negative feelings or emotions by helping you become more self-aware. It can sharpen the mind, reduce stress and even increase your concentration levels and attention span. Daily meditation is like exercise for the brain and will increase the strength and endurance of your focus levels over time. Meditation is perfect medication for your overall mental health!

Being able to maintain and manage our emotions is one of the biggest benefits of meditation. It brings a sense of calm, peace and balance to the soul. It also can assist by increasing the positive energy of your emotions and allow you to have more control over them. It is not encouraged to try and meditate when you're feeling angry, upset or overwhelmed. Rather, once you are ready to create a calm environment for yourself, meditation provides an emotional release by encouraging us to cope with life in a more beneficial way. Please note, that sometimes meditation can bring out inner emotions that have not yet healed from trauma or past life experiences. It's important to feel *everything* during the process of meditation and not resist it. I have found that in my deepest meditations, tears naturally purge themselves externally, while my emotions are balancing internally. This type of discharge is a natural and holistic way to disperse feelings or emotions that are hindering the development of your inner peace.

The physical benefits of meditation are endless! It can improve your overall health especially when it comes to matters of the heart and lungs. It can change how you perceive and respond to physical pain. Meditation improves digestion and can enhance the function of your GI tract and rates of metabolism. In my personal opinion, the organ benefiting the most from meditation would be your brain. It can increase the capacity and mass of the hippocampus which is vital for memory. Your blood pressure decreases during meditation and lowers overtime for people who meditate regularly. Breathwork during meditation can also increase the elasticity and strength of your lungs. See, I told you the physical benefits are endless!

Regular meditation can help alleviate the effects of anxiety on the body as well. Mindfulness meditation may also help to decrease cognitive decline from aging or Alzheimer's. It reduces stress on the heart and blood vessels which can also help prevent heart disease. By reducing our stress levels this decreases amounts of adrenaline and cortisol in our systems. This means that meditation may also be extremely beneficial in fighting cancer and other physical diseases or ailments.

Finally, spiritually speaking, meditation is access to our soul and all its wonder. It is a place where we can connect to something higher, whether it be (Mother Father) God, Source, Spirit or the Universe in general. Meditation is an opportunity to commune with our spirit and be in tune with that inner self we all have. In all my years of education and encounters as a medium, I believe we are spiritual beings having a human experience. By honoring our body, mind and soul with meditation, we provide the spiritual sunshine and watering needed to thrive and feel fully connected to this earthly journey called 'life'. Remember, meditation is medication for the soul.

In conclusion, I have found meditation to be extremely beneficial in so many ways while learning, exploring and practicing it. I honestly believe that making meditation a daily routine will dramatically change your life for the better. It has been proven over time, with much education and research, that meditation is one of the most valuable practices we can commit to in our lives. Crossing boundaries of religion, wealth and culture, meditation is great for every soul from every background. As I have stated multiple times already, it has become my personal mantra over the years to say that "meditation is the best medication". Beginning to learn about and practice meditation as early as childhood, or even later into adulthood, can only result in a lifetime of positive mental, emotional and physical health for all.

For it was finding my strength and spirit thought
meditation, that I continue to awaken...

Conclusion

Find your Light

"The light that guides you shines from within."

– Rumi

One thing I know for sure is that we never stop learning, it's impossible to know everything about everything in our lifetime here. My hope is that by focusing on the topics discussed in this book it will benefit your time spent on earth and hopefully make it a little easier to navigate. It's going to be a challenge here, that is guaranteed! I wish I could say that I live by these guidelines being presented every moment of my life, but that would be untruthful. I'm still a work in progress, like most of us are. I have days where I don't follow my own advice, then once I get back on track and identify the deeper issues, things start to work themselves out. I've noticed that redirecting myself is half of the battle, even calling myself out for needlessly focusing my energy on the stress in life that does not matter. It is part of the process! Talk to yourself in a positive way internally and externally as needed, because sometimes the best thing you can hear is what YOU say to YOU.

The journey of awakening does not happen overnight or instantly. It takes time and many lessons learned until we finally get to the point when we discover the purpose in all of it. It's so healthy to recognize and recall *all* the ups, downs, good days and tough times that helped to mold you into the badass, beautiful soul you are today. Enlightenment finally happens when you can appreciate and accept all that's been given to you up to this point in your life. Then continue to look forward and make the best of what time remains with all that you have learned.

As I continue to embrace the path of enlightenment, there's something that I have discovered throughout all these years, that I believe to be true. I share this belief openly with no intention of changing anyone's feelings or faith. The following statements have been validated to me through my own education, experiences and observations. I believe, that 'God' is not a designated deity to one singular religion. Nor is it some old man with a beard high above us calling all the shots and guiding our lives. What I have learned of God is that it is a genderless, ceaseless energy source of light that is inside every single one of us. The same light that makes up the stars in the universe - is within you. (To my science fiction friends who are nerds like my brothers, consider God to be exactly like 'the force' in Star Wars!) This light has always been there, and even though it may have gotten lost or dim at times, it never truly goes away. This is a constant flow of energy that responds to high and low vibrations like everything else. Once you find it, you will never let the darkness take over again. Igniting your inner light becomes easier over time and with experience, because you know exactly where to find it when it starts to fade. You also figure out who or what lights you up most, be grateful for that connection and what it or they have brought to your life.

After going through all that I have experienced to get to this point of my awakening, I have found that maintaining a focus on the positive around me is what brightens my light within me the most. For each of us it will be different, but for me it is my children, family and friends, mediumship, helping others, laughter, travel, babies, music, nature, warm chocolate chip cookies, animals, random acts of kindness and the comfort of my own bed at night. When you can concentrate on what brings pure joy to your soul, you will find your light and shine brighter than you ever have before.

My purpose in writing this book was to help whoever may be reading it to know that you are not alone. We all have feelings of despair and hopelessness at times in our lives that feel so overwhelming. It is learning how to cope and deal with them in a positive way that we can change our lives for the better. That by understanding energy, releasing our fears, offering forgiveness for ourselves and others, acknowledging the law of attraction and practicing daily meditation - you can have a wonderful, peaceful and healing human experience. My final wish for anyone reading this is that through my own personal stories of enlightenment, pain, chaos and joy – you will feel inspired to create the life you have always wanted and deserved.

For when you find your light, you will awaken.

THE END